BLACK & DECKER ®

THE COMPLETE GUIDE TO
FLOORING

Design, Planning & Installation
for All Types of Flooring

Creative Publishing
international

CHANHASSEN, MINNESOTA
www.creativepub.com

Contents

FLOORING PLANNING & PREPARATION

**Creative Publishing
international**

Copyright © 2003
Creative Publishing international, Inc.
18705 Lake Drive East
Chanhassen, Minnesota 55317
1-800-328-3895
www.creativepub.com
All rights reserved

Printed in China

10 9 8 7 6

President/CEO: Ken Fund
Vice President/Publisher: Linda Ball
Vice President/Retail Sales & Marketing: Kevin Haas

Executive Editor: Bryan Trandem
Creative Director: Tim Himsel
Managing Editor: Michelle Skudlarek
Editorial Director: Jerri Farris

Lead Editor: Brett Martin
Copy Editor: Karen Ruth
Proofreader: Shannon Zemlicka
Senior Art Director: David Schelitzche
Mac Designer: Jon Simpson
Project Manager: Tracy Stanley
Illustrators: David Schelitzche, Jon Simpson, Earl Slack
Photo Researchers: Julie Caruso, Andrew Karre
Studio Services Manager: Jeanette Moss McCurdy
Photographers: Tate Carlson, Andrea Rugg
Photo Stylists: Joanne Wawra, Theresa Henn
Scene Shop Carpenter: Randy Austin
Director, Production Services & Photography: Kim Gerber
Production Manager: Stasia Dorn

THE COMPLETE GUIDE TO FLOORING
Created by: The Editors of Creative Publishing international, Inc., in
cooperation with Black & Decker. Black & Decker® is a trademark of
The Black & Decker Corporation and is used under license.

Library of Congress
Cataloging-in-Publication Data

The Complete guide to flooring : design, planning & installation for all types of flooring /
  Black & Decker.
    p. cm.
    Includes index.
    ISBN 1-58923-092-2
    1. Flooring--Handbooks, manuals, etc. 2. Floors--Maintenance and repair--Handbooks, manuals, etc. I. Black & Decker Corporation (Towson, Md.)

TH2525.C65 2003
690'.16--dc21

2003053111

Portions of *The Complete Guide to Flooring* are taken from the Black & Decker® books *Flooring Projects & Techniques; The Complete Guide to Painting & Decorating; The Complete Photo Guide to Home Repair; The Complete Photo Guide to Home Improvement; Building Your Outdoor Home;* Other titles from Creative Publishing international include:

The New Everyday Home Repairs; Basic Wiring & Electrical Repairs; Building Decks; Home Masonry Projects & Repairs; Workshop Tips & Techniques; Bathroom Remodeling; Customizing Your Home; Carpentry: Remodeling; Carpentry: Tools • Shelves • Walls • Doors; Exterior Home Repairs & Improvements, Home Plumbing Projects & Repairs; Advanced Home Wiring; Advanced Deck Building; Built-In Projects for the Home; Landscape Design & Construction; Refinishing & Finishing Wood; Building Porches & Patios; Advanced Home Plumbing; Remodeling Kitchens; Finishing Basements & Attics; Stonework & Masonry Projects; Sheds, Gazebos & Outbuildings; Building & Finishing Walls & Ceilings; The Complete Guide to Home Plumbing; The Complete Guide to Home Wiring; The Complete Guide to Building Decks; The Complete Guide to Creative Landscapes; The Complete Guide to Home Masonry; The Complete Guide to Home Carpentry; The Complete Guide to Home Storage; The Complete Guide to Windows & Doors; The Complete Guide to Bathrooms; Complete Guide to Ceramic & Stone Tile; Accessible Home; Open House; Lighting Design & Installation; The Complete Photo Guide to Outdoor Home Improvement.

Introduction

If you're like most homeowners, you concentrate on the wall décor and furnishings in a room without fully considering the importance of the floor. In reality, there's no better way to liven up a room and give it new character than to change the flooring.

Because it's one of the largest elements in a room, a floor creates instant impact, and today's products make installing your own brand-new floor easier than ever. Installing a new floor also offers some of the greatest rewards for the money and time invested.

Floors serve a much larger purpose beyond merely providing a walking surface and a place to rest furniture. All by itself, a floor helps to create a room's mood by adding color, texture, style, and personality. A tired living room with worn carpeting becomes a stylish parlor with the addition of gleaming new laminate plank flooring. You can make a cold basement room with an old resilient tile floor an attractive recreation room by adding plush carpet. An outdated kitchen with linoleum flooring becomes the heart of the home with the installation of textured ceramic tile with a radiant in-floor heating system.

A quality floor can complement a room's décor and offer a feeling of continuity, or it can provide a contrast to its surroundings and draw attention to individual components in a room. Either way, flooring plays a vital role in the look and feel of your home. Few room elements have this kind of impact, so whether you're remodeling an entire room or making minor adjustments, consider updating your floor to add some charisma to the finished project.

The Complete Guide to Flooring helps you choose and install the floor that best suits your needs. There's a seemingly infinite number of possibilities when it comes to flooring options, from exotic hardwoods to traditional woods, from ceramic to stone, vinyl to leather, rubber to cork, not to mention all the possibilities afforded by combining two or more coverings in a room.

The first section of this book, Planning & Designing Your New Floor, features a portfolio of flooring ideas to assist you in planning your new floor and selecting a covering that enriches your room. You'll probably find some exciting ideas that you haven't considered.

Before installing your new floor, some preparation is required. The entire second section is devoted to removing old flooring and preparing your subfloor. You'll also learn how to install various underlayments, including soundproofing, to ensure a durable finished floor.

At the core of *The Complete Guide to Flooring* are the installation processes for the most common, decorative, and stylish floor coverings on today's market. The sections on floor installation provide detailed, step-by-step instructions and color photos for installing wood floors, including tongue-and-groove hardwoods, parquets, floating floors, and end grain; ceramic, stone, and resilient coverings; and carpeting. Not only will you learn installation techniques, you'll discover how to give your floors a custom look using the same procedures as professional installers.

Another section in the book explains how to apply finishes to your floor and add your own unique borders. This section gives you ideas for bringing an existing floor back to life.

If your floors or stairs are squeaking or damaged, the final section of the book can help. It serves as a guide for repairing and maintaining your floors. Keep this book on hand as a reference in case you experience squeaky floors or need to replace a tile, a patch of carpet or vinyl, or a strip or two of wood.

NOTICE TO READERS

For safety, use caution, care, and good judgment when following the procedures described in this book. Neither the Publisher nor Black & Decker® can assume responsibility for any damage to property or injury to persons as a result of misuse of the information provided.

Consult your local Building Department for information on building permits, codes, and other laws as they apply to your project.

Planning & Designing Your New Floor

Like any successful remodeling project, replacing your floor covering requires careful planning and attention to design. Flooring is not autonomous. It should fit into the overall design of the room to create a desired effect. If you choose, the floor can create excitement and become a focal point. Or you can install a floor that serves as a background for the rest of the room and doesn't draw attention.

Through careful planning, you can choose flooring that can be used successfully in multiple rooms, or select a pattern or design that's repeated throughout the room or in adjacent rooms.

Keep in mind that your flooring design will last a long time, especially if you're installing ceramic tile or wood. In most cases, the only way to change the design of your floor is to install a new floor covering. The design you choose is there to stay for a long time, so plan accordingly.

The information in this section will help you plan and design floors that meet your needs. After looking through the portfolio section for ideas of various floor coverings, you may also want to visit a flooring showroom to find the color, style, and pattern of the material you want to use.

Decorations create excitement in floors and provide a focal point in the room. The hardwood floor on the left features a decorative medallion that adds character to the foyer. The floor above sets off the dining area with a bold border around the edge of the room.

Compare flooring samples, available from flooring distributors, to see which looks best with your room colors and furnishings. If you plan to repaint walls, use color chips to pick colors that will complement your new floor.

Planning Your New Floor

Because floors are highly visible, appearance is one of the most important considerations when choosing flooring. Start your search by browsing through magazines and visiting flooring retail stores.

There are other characteristics besides appearance to keep in mind when choosing a floor covering. Cost and ease of installation are key concerns for most people. For others, durability and how the flooring feels underfoot are important factors.

In a room subject to moisture, heavy traffic, or other special conditions, consider how different floor coverings will perform under these situations. Some flooring cannot be installed in moisture areas, while others can fade or scuff under heavy traffic. See the comparisons on pages 10 and 11 for help in choosing a floor covering that best fits your needs.

When estimating materials for your project, add 5 to 10% to your total square footage to allow for waste caused by trimming. For some carpet installations, you'll need to add even more. After your project is completed, save any extra flooring material in case future repairs are required.

Planning a Flooring Project

Establish a logical work sequence. Many flooring projects are done as part of a more comprehensive remodeling project. In this case, the flooring should be installed after the walls and ceiling are finished, but before the fixtures are installed. Protect new flooring with heavy paper or tarps when completing your remodeling project.

Measure the area of the project room to calculate the quantity of materials you'll need. Measure the full width and length of the space to determine the overall square footage, then subtract the square footage of areas that will not be covered, such as stairways, cabinets, and other permanent fixtures. Add 5 to 10% to the total to allow for waste.

Checklist for Planning a Flooring Project

Read the following sections and use this checklist to organize your activities as you start your flooring project.

❑ Measure the project area carefully. Be sure to include all nooks and closets as well as areas under all movable appliances. Calculate the total square footage of the project area.

❑ Use your measurements to create a floor plan on graph paper.

❑ Sketch pattern options on tracing paper laid over the floor plan to help you visualize what the flooring will look like when it's installed.

❑ Identify areas where the type of floor covering will change, and choose the best threshold material to use for the transition.

❑ Estimate the amount of preparation material needed, including underlayment sheets and floor leveler.

❑ Estimate the amount of installation material needed, including the floor covering and other supplies, such as adhesives, grouts, thresholds, tackless strips, and screws. For help in estimating, go to a building supply center and read the labels on materials and adhesives to determine coverage.

❑ Make a list of the tools needed for the job. Locate sources for the tools you'll need to buy or rent.

❑ Estimate the total cost of the project, including all preparation materials, flooring and installation materials, and tools. For expensive materials, comparison-shop to get the best prices.

❑ Check with building supply centers or flooring retail stores for delivery costs. Delivery service is often inexpensive and well worth the additional charge.

❑ Determine how much demolition you'll need to do, and plan for debris removal, either through your regular garbage collector or a disposal company.

❑ Plan for the temporary displacement of furnishings and removable appliances to minimize disruption of your daily routine.

Choosing a Floor Covering

Vinyl Flooring

Vinyl flooring, also known as "resilient flooring," is a versatile, flexible surface that can be used almost anywhere, although it's most often found in kitchens and bathrooms. Vinyl flooring is available in both sheets and tiles, in thicknesses ranging from $\frac{1}{16}$" to $\frac{1}{8}$". Sheets come in 6-ft.-wide or 12-ft.-wide rolls, with either a felt or a polyvinyl chloride (PVC) backing, depending on the type of installation. Tiles typically come in 12" squares and are available with or without self-adhesive backing.

Installation is easy. Sheet vinyl with felt backing is glued to the floor using the full-spread method, meaning the entire project area is covered with adhesive. PVC-backed sheet vinyl is glued only along the edges (perimeter-bond method). Tiles are the easiest to install, but because tile floors have a lot of seams, they're less suitable for high-moisture areas. All vinyl flooring must be installed over a smooth underlayment.

Sheet vinyl is priced per square yard, while tile is priced per square foot. Cost for either style is comparable to carpet and less expensive than ceramic tile or hardwood. Prices vary based on the percentage of vinyl in the material, the thickness of the product, and the complexity of the pattern.

Ceramic Tile

Ceramic tile is a hard, durable, versatile material that's available in a wide variety of sizes, patterns, shapes, and colors. This all-purpose flooring is an excellent choice for high traffic and high moisture areas. It's commonly used in bathrooms, entryways, and kitchens.

Common ceramic tiles include unglazed quarry tile, glazed ceramic tile, and porcelain mosaic tile. As an alternative to ceramic tiles, natural stone tiles are available in several materials, including marble, slate, and granite. Thicknesses for most floor tiles range from $\frac{3}{16}$" to $\frac{3}{4}$".

In general, ceramic tile is more expensive than other types of floor coverings, with natural stone tile ranking as the most expensive. While tile is more time-consuming to install than other materials, it offers the most flexibility of design.

Floor preparation is critical to the success of a tile installation. In high moisture areas, such as bathrooms, tile should be laid over a cementboard underlayment that's fastened to the subfloor. All floors that support tile must be stiff and flat to prevent cracking in the tile surface. Tile is installed following a grid-pattern layout and adhered to the floor with thin-set mortar. The gaps between individual tiles are filled with grout, which should be sealed periodically to prevent staining.

Wood Flooring

Wood floors are resilient and durable, yet they still look warm and elegant. They hold up well in high-traffic areas and are popular in dining rooms, living rooms, and entryways.

Traditional solid wood planks are the most common type of wood flooring, but there's a growing selection of plywood backed and synthetic-laminate products (also called laminated wood) that are well suited for do-it-yourself installation. Oak and maple are the most common wood species available, and size options include narrow strips, wide planks, and parquet squares. Most wood flooring has tongue-and-groove construction, which helps to provide a strong, flat surface.

In general, hardwood flooring is slightly less expensive than ceramic tile, and laminated products are typically less expensive than solid hardwood. Most types of wood flooring can be installed directly over a subfloor and sometimes over vinyl flooring. Installation of laminated wood flooring is simple. It can be glued or nailed down, or "floated" on a foam cushion. Parquet squares typically are glued down. Solid hardwood planks must be nailed to the subfloor.

Carpet

Carpet is a soft, flexible floor covering that's chosen primarily for comfort rather than durability. It's a popular choice for bedrooms, family rooms, and hallways.

Carpet is made of synthetic or natural fibers bonded to a mesh backing and usually sold in 12-ft.-wide rolls. Some types have a cushioned backing, ready for glue-down installation without pads or strips.

The two basic types of carpeting are loop-pile, which is made with uncut loops of yarn to create texture, and cut-pile, which has trimmed fibers for a more uniform appearance. Some carpets contain both types. Carpet is similar in price to vinyl flooring, but costs vary depending on density and fiber. Wool is typically more expensive than synthetics.

Installing carpet is not difficult, but it does involve some special tools and techniques. Tackless strips and padding are installed, then the carpeting is cut and seamed, and secured to the tackless strips.

Flooring for Safe & Easy Movement

Choosing the best flooring for multi-generational use in families usually involves compromise. For example, carpet reduces noise and is safer in case of accidents, but hard flooring is better for wheelchair movement. Here are some tips to consider when weighing your options:

- Floor coverings of different thicknesses can create rough transitions between rooms. Try to keep floor levels consistent, and use low-profile transition strips where necessary.
- Natural wood floors and solid vinyl flooring with a matte finish may offer the best traction.
- Non-slip flooring is best for kitchens and bathrooms. Ask a flooring dealer about the coefficient of friction, which should be at least .6.

- Area rugs can be unsafe unless they are secured to the floor.
- Low-pile carpet (¼" to ½") reduces the risk of tripping and provides a better surface for wheelchairs than high-pile carpet.
- Cushion-backed carpet can reduce carpet rippling and drag caused by wheelchairs.
- Lightly textured tile is better for wheelchairs than tile with a smooth finish. Avoid wide grout joints with any type of tile.

Design Tips for Flooring

No matter what type of floor you're installing, choose your colors, patterns, and textures carefully since it's likely you'll be living with your selection for many years—or even decades. Flooring is one of the most visible and important elements of all interior design.

Flooring can serve as a bold, eye-catching design statement, or it can be an understated background, but whatever approach you take, always consider the design of the adjoining rooms when choosing flooring. Because floors flow from one room to the next, floor coverings offer a convenient medium for creating continuity throughout your home. This doesn't mean you should use the same floor covering in every room. Simply repeating a color, pattern, or texture often is enough to provide continuity.

The examples on these pages help illustrate how your choice of color, pattern, and texture can affect the look and feel of a room.

Design continuity can be provided by using the same flooring in adjacent rooms. The living room and hallway shown above left are joined by the same pattern and color scheme in the cork flooring. The entryway and hallway on the left are joined by square ceramic tiles and a border laid in a ruglike pattern.

Color of flooring influences the visual impact of a room. Bold, bright colors draw attention, while muted colors create a neutral background that doesn't compete for attention. Colors also affect the perceived size of a room. Dark colors are formal in tone, but can make a room look smaller. Light colors are more contemporary, and can make the room seem larger.

Pattern of flooring affects the feeling and tone of a room. In general, subtle patterns lend a more relaxed feel to a room and can make it appear larger. Bold, recurring patterns create excitement and focal points for a room. A flooring pattern must be chosen carefully to ensure it doesn't clash with other patterns in the room.

Texture of flooring contributes to the style of a room. More rugged surfaces, such as slate or berber carpet, give a room a warm, earthy tone. Smooth and glossy surfaces, such as polished marble tile or hardwood flooring, impart an airy sense of elegance.

A Gallery of Flooring Ideas

The perfect floor is an integral component of any interior design. A well-chosen floor covering will interact with other design elements in the room. The flooring should also be practical and fit the needs of each room. For example, in a kitchen where spills are common, sheet vinyl or ceramic tile is a more practical choice than

These rooms each feature two floor coverings. The main floors are hardwood, then a carpet or rug is placed under the seating areas to provide comfort underfoot. These hardwoods complement the second floor coverings and accent the wood accessories in the rooms.

expensive, deep-pile wool car-pet. In a formal dining room, parquet is more fitting than re-silient tiles.

The impressive photos in this section highlight a wide range of flooring types and materials for any room in the home. You're sure to find new ideas for ways to meet your flooring needs.

Photo courtesy of Marmoleum by Forbo Linoleum

Photo courtesy of Wilsonart Flooring

The dark colors in the checkerboard floor at the top not only contrast with each other, but they help anchor and "ground" the overwhelmingly light color scheme of this setting. The light color in the floor above provides the right balance to the darker walls.

Hardwood

Hardwood strips and planks are the most common wood floor coverings. Hardwood doesn't compete with ornate elements in a room, yet it makes a definitive statement. The floor above uses two different woods to create an appealing border around the kitchen island. The floor on the right blends with the fireplace mantel, bookshelves, and wall panels to establish an elegant, old-world look.

Parquet floors are higher-end hardwood floor coverings that create decorative, and sometimes intricate, patterns. The herringbone pattern above uses narrow strips of wood set at right angles to each other to form an intriguing design. The parquet floor on the left uses wood tiles to create an attractive, three-dimensional look.

Photo courtesy of Kentucky Wood Floors

17

Laminate

Laminate floors often look like solid wood, and they resist scratching, denting, and fading. Laminate floors are available in different colors and textures to resemble different wood species. The floor on the left offers the warmth and beauty of hardwood, and because it's laminate, it works well in a bathroom. The floor below mimics the look of rich, natural wood planks, but it's actually laminated flooring.

Laminate floors that replicate the look of ceramic tile are hard to distinguish from genuine ceramic. The laminate floors to the right and below look almost identical to ceramic tile.

Ceramic Tile

Tiles on floors and walls can work together to create a look and mood for the entire kitchen (right). This floor uses different sizes of tile to create a serene pattern that doesn't compete with the pattern on the walls.

The earth tones in the tile below provide a subtle background for the light, natural look of the room.

Square and rectangular ceramic tiles (left) can be combined for a sleek, contemporary look.

Irregular shapes give floors a rustic look (below). The flooring continues into the adjacent rooms to provide continuity.

Resilient

A checkerboard pattern is a common floor design. The resilient floor on the left combines several subdued colors for a more contemporary look, while the floor below uses black and white colors for maximum contrast.

Sheet vinyl offers a uniquely decorative covering not possible with other flooring. This floor provides color to an otherwise monochrome room.

Moisture resistant and easy to clean, vinyl is a practical and attractive choice for this kitchen. The floor imitates the look of slate, but is slightly cushioned, making it less fatiguing to stand on.

Cork makes a great-looking floor covering, provides comfort underfoot, and reduces noise in a room. It's also environmentally friendly. The bark of a cork oak tree naturally splits every 9 to 15 years and can be harvested without harming the tree. Cork oak trees can reach the age of 250 years old. Cork floor is available in different colors and patterns.

Photo of Expanko Rubber Flooring courtesy of Expanko , Inc.

Environmentally Friendly

Rubber floors are a good choice for basements and exercise areas. If you're concerned about the environment, check with the manufacturer to make sure the flooring is made with recycled rubber. Rubber flooring is available in a wide range of colors to fit your room's décor. This floor features rubber and cork.

Photo courtesy of TimberGrass LLC

Bamboo is actually a grass, not a tree. The bamboo is harvested every three to five years and continues to regenerate, making it an ecologically friendly flooring. Bamboo is easily identifiable by its distinctive grain, or "knuckles," and is available in strips and in planks.

25

Carpet

Wall-to-wall carpet is very versatile and easily adopts the style and feel of the other room elements that surround it. The carpet in the family room above takes on a sophisticated, yet comfortable, look. The carpet on the left reflects the quiet, more subdued feeling of the living room.

Dense plush carpet creates a feeling of relaxation that's right at home in private quarters.

Shag is still fashionable, as in this living area. The carpet color matches the couch and walls.

This elegant carpet lends itself to the contemporary look and feel of the room. The carpet provides comfort underfoot, yet it also looks attractive in this setting.

Luxurious

For homeowners who want a truly luxurious floor covering, leather is the perfect choice. It offers a very distinctive look and feel that can't be replicated by less expensive imitations. The floor above is composed of tiles, the floor in the middle on the right features leather flooring in a herringbone pattern, while the floor on the bottom right is textured.

End grain floors, which are composed of wood "bricks," also offer a luxurious covering. This high-end flooring (right) is sure to impress even the most discriminating homeowner and turn the floor into a work of art. The above photos show end grain patterns for flooring.

Outdoor Floors

Don't overlook the outdoors when planning floor coverings. An attractive outdoor floor adds to the pleasure of sitting outside. The tile floor on the right features a decorative border with the field tile installed diagonally for added effect. The flooring also complements the exterior wall tile. A two-tone brick herringbone on the floor below makes this deck more appealing.

This sleek outdoor floor (above) repeats the look of the materials used on the house to offer an inviting entrance into the home. The floor on the right offers a relaxing patio area. Both floors look perfectly natural in their outdoor surroundings.

Combination Floors

Using two or more floor coverings in combination offers a striking look that can't be achieved with a single floor type. The bamboo wood floor above is joined by tile from an adjacent room, tile around the fireplace, and carpet leading up the stairs. The hardwood floor to the right is partially covered by a plush rug for added comfort and an appealing look.

Area rugs are a great addition to any floor. They can be placed over all floor coverings to add a decorative touch to a room. The red rug matches the red accessories in the room, while the neutral carpet underneath matches the white in the couch and walls.

Determining the number and type of coverings already on your floor is an important early evaluation step. Too many layers of flooring and underlayment can stress floor joists and ultimately cause a new floor to fail. An easy way to check for old flooring is to remove floor vents.

Evaluating an Existing Floor

The first step in preparing for a new floor covering is evaluating your old floor. A careful examination can help you decide whether to repair damaged areas or to replace the flooring altogether.

Evaluating your floor is a three-step process. Begin by identifying the existing floor material and the installation method used. Is your sheet vinyl attached using the full-spread method or the perimeter-bond method? Is your carpet glued down or stretched? Next, assess the condition of the floor. Is it securely attached or is it loose in spots? Is it chipped or cracked? Finally, note the height of the existing floor in relation to adjoining floor surfaces. Is it significantly higher than surrounding floors?

Often, a new floor covering or underlayment can be installed on top of existing flooring. If the existing flooring is not sound or smooth, however, you'll have to do some preparation work. A simple modification to your existing floor may be to apply a floor leveler (see page 55). More complex preparations may involve removing and replacing the underlayment (see pages 52 to 53, 58 to 61) or making spot repairs to the subfloor (see page 55). Avoid taking shortcuts since this usually results in an inferior floor.

Warning: Resilient flooring manufactured before 1986 may contain asbestos, which can cause severe lung problems if inhaled. The recommended method for dealing with asbestos-laden flooring is to cover it with an underlayment. If the flooring must be removed, do not do the work yourself. Instead, consult a certified asbestos-abatement contractor.

Anatomy of Your Floor

A typical wood-frame floor consists of several layers that work together to provide the required structural support and desired appearance. At the bottom of the floor are the joists, the 2 × 10 or larger framing members that support the weight of the floor. Joists are typically spaced 16" apart on center. The subfloor is nailed to the joists. Most subfloors installed in the 1970s or later are made of ¾" tongue and groove plywood, but in older homes, the subfloor often consists of 1"-thick wood planks nailed diagonally across the floor joists. On top of the subfloor, most builders place a ½" plywood underlayment. For many types of floor coverings, adhesive or mortar is spread on the underlayment prior to installing the floor covering.

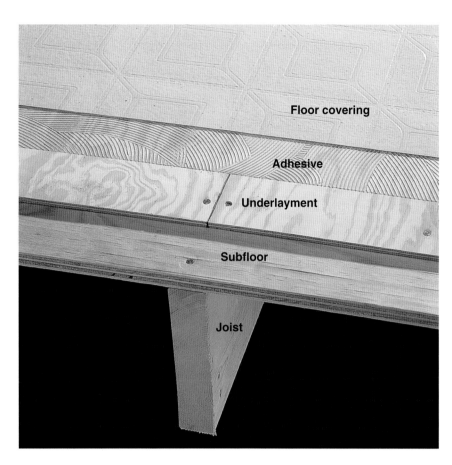

Floor covering

Adhesive

Underlayment

Subfloor

Joist

Tips for Evaluating Floors

When installing new flooring over old, measure vertical spaces to make sure enclosed or under-counter appliances will fit once the new underlayment and flooring are installed. Use samples of the new underlayment and floor covering as spacers when measuring.

High thresholds often indicate that several layers of flooring have already been installed on top of one another. If you have several layers, it's best to remove them before installing the new floor covering.

(continued next page)

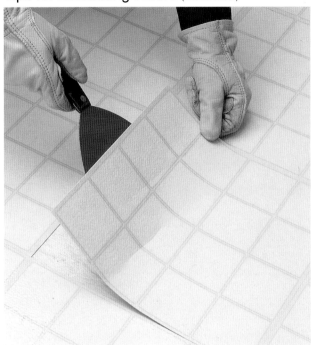

Loose tiles may indicate widespread failure of the adhesive. Use a wallboard knife to test tiles. If tiles can be pried up easily in many different areas of the room, plan to remove all of the flooring.

Air bubbles trapped under resilient sheet flooring indicate that the adhesive has failed. The old flooring must be removed before the new covering can be installed.

Cracks in grout joints around ceramic tile are a sign that movement of the floor covering has caused, or has been caused by, deterioration of the adhesive layer. If more than 10% of the tiles are loose, remove the old flooring. Evaluate the condition of the underlayment (see opposite page) to determine if it also must be removed.

Buckling in solid hardwood floors indicates that the boards have loosened from the subfloor. Do not remove hardwood floors. Instead, refasten loose boards by drilling pilot holes and inserting flooring nails or screws. New carpet can be installed right over a well-fastened hardwood floor. New ceramic tile or resilient flooring should be installed over underlayment placed on the hardwood flooring.

A Quick Guide for Evaluating Your Existing Floor

Preparing for a new floor can be a simple task or a lengthy, difficult chore, depending on the condition of the existing floor and your choice of new floor coverings.

The following descriptions summarize the preparation steps for various types of existing floor materials. In some cases, you have several preparation options from which to choose. By carefully considering the options and choosing the most suitable method for your needs, you can avoid wasting time with unnecessary labor. Keep in mind that the goal of any preparation for new flooring is the creation of a structurally sound, smooth, and level surface.

Old Resilient (Vinyl) Flooring

Option 1: Your existing resilient floor can serve as the foundation for most new floor coverings, including resilient flooring, hardwood, and carpet, but only if the existing surface is relatively smooth and sound. Inspect the existing flooring for loose seams, tears, chips, air bubbles, and other areas where the bond has failed. If these loose spots constitute less than 30% of the total area, you can remove the flooring at these spots and fill the voids with floor-leveling compound. Then, apply embossing leveler to the entire floor and let it dry before laying new resilient flooring.

Option 2: If the original resilient flooring is suspect, you can install new underlayment over the old surface after repairing obviously loose areas.

Option 3: If you're installing ceramic tile, or if the existing surface is in very poor condition, the old resilient flooring should be removed entirely before you install new flooring. If the old flooring was glued down with full-bond adhesive, it's usually easiest to remove both the flooring and underlayment at the same time. If the old underlayment is removed, you must install new underlayment before laying the new flooring.

Old Ceramic Tile

Option 1: If the existing ceramic tile surface is relatively solid, new flooring usually can be laid directly over the tile. Inspect tiles and joints for cracks and loose pieces. Remove loose material and fill these areas with a floor-leveling compound. If you're installing resilient flooring, apply an embossing leveler product over the ceramic tile before laying the new flooring. If you're laying new ceramic tile over the old surface, use an epoxy-based thin-set mortar for better adhesion.

Option 2: If more than 10% of the tiles are loose, remove all of the old flooring before installing the new surface. If the tiles don't easily separate from the underlayment, it's best to remove the tile and the underlayment at the same time, then install new underlayment.

Old Hardwood Flooring

Option 1: If you're installing carpet, you can usually lay it directly over an existing hardwood floor, provided it's a nailed or glued-down surface. Inspect the flooring and secure any loose areas to the subfloor with spiral-shanked flooring nails, then remove any rotted wood and fill the voids with floor-leveling compound before installing the carpet.

Option 2: If you're installing resilient flooring or ceramic tile over nailed hardwood planks or glued-down wood flooring, you can attach new underlayment over the existing hardwood before installing the new flooring.

Option 3: If the existing floor is a "floating" wood or laminate surface with a foam-pad underlayment, remove it completely before laying any type of new flooring.

Underlayment & Subfloor

Underlayment must be smooth, solid, and level to ensure a long-lasting flooring installation. If the existing underlayment does not meet these standards, remove it and install new underlayment before you lay new flooring.

Before installing new underlayment, inspect the subfloor for chips, open knots, dips, and loose boards. Screw down loose areas, and fill cracks and dips with floor-leveling compound. Remove and replace any water-damaged areas.

Old Carpet

Without exception, carpet must be removed before you install any new flooring. For traditional carpet, simply cut the carpet into pieces, then remove the padding and the tackless strips. Remove glued-down cushion-back carpet with a floor scraper, using the same techniques as for removing full-bond resilient sheet flooring (see page 49).

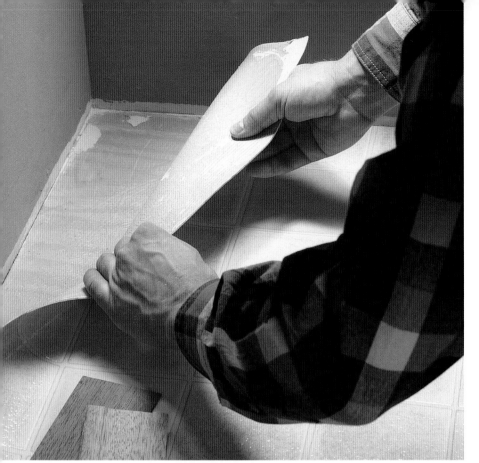

Installing a New Floor: A Step-by-Step Overview

Understanding the separate phases of a flooring installation and their relationship to one another will help you manage the job better from start to finish. The sequence shown on these pages will give you a basic overview of a typical installation, though your project may deviate from this sequence.

If your flooring installation is part of a larger remodeling project, schedule the flooring phase as part of the overall remodeling project.

1 Once you've selected a new flooring to install, evaluate your existing floor to determine whether or not you can install the new flooring over it (pages 34 to 37).

2 If necessary, remove the existing flooring to provide a sound surface for your new floor installation (pages 48 to 53).

3 Install the appropriate type of underlayment for your floor covering (pages 54 to 61).

4 Lay out your floor for installation. For resilient or ceramic tile, establish layout lines that divide the room into quadrants (pages 135 to 136). For sheet vinyl, create a template of the room perimeter (page 129). For carpet, determine the positions of seams (page 176).

5 Install your floor covering using the appropriate techniques: resilient flooring (pages 130 to 139), ceramic tile (pages 148 to 155), tongue-and-groove hardwood flooring (pages 94 to 99), parquet flooring (pages 104 to 107), end grain floors (pages 110 to 113), floating floors (pages 118 to 121), and carpet (pages 186 to 197).

Project Preparation

Before your new floor goes in, your old floor will probably need to be taken out and the subfloor carefully prepared for a finished surface. Project preparation is just as important as installing your floor covering and requires the same attention to detail.

Don't assume that because your subfloor will be covered, the covering will hide imperfections in the subfloor. In most cases, those flaws will only be accentuated in the finished floor, especially with resilient surfaces.

Removing old floors, installing new subfloors or underlayments, and filling in cracks and joints isn't the most glamorous job in the world, but it's an investment that will reap big rewards when your flooring project is complete.

If your new floor is part of a larger home improvement project, removing the existing floor is one of the first steps in the overall project, while installing the new floor is one of the last steps in the process. All other demolition and construction should be finished in the room before the floor is installed to avoid damaging the surface.

The projects in this section show you how to remove floor coverings, including sheet vinyl, ceramic tiles, and carpet; repair subfloors; install underlayment; and prepare basement floors. You'll also learn how to install an electrical outlet in your floor to make plugging in appliances more convenient, and how to install in-floor heating to keep your floors warm and toasty.

Project Preparation

Project preparation can range from simple to complex, depending on the condition of your existing floor. As a guide for making preparation decisions, evaluate your floor following the process shown on pages 34 to 37.

Providing a sound, smooth underlayment for your new flooring is a vital preparation step. This may involve only minor modifications to your existing floor, such as applying an embossing leveler, or the preparation may require complete underlayment removal and spot repairs to your subfloor. Avoid taking shortcuts because they usually result in an inferior floor.

If you're installing new underlayment, it's essential that you choose the right material. There are several types of underlayment available, so make sure to select one that's recommended for your flooring type.

Before getting started on your floor preparation project, remove all appliances and bathroom fixtures from the room to make the working conditions as efficient and comfortable as possible. This will also eliminate the possibility of damaging the appliances during the preparation process.

Be sure to take proper safety precautions and wear safety goggles, work gloves, work boots, and a dust particle mask when doing preparation work.

Options for Removing Old Flooring

Remove the floor covering only. If the underlayment is sturdy and in good condition, you can usually get by with simply scraping off the floor covering, then cleaning and reusing the existing underlayment.

Remove the floor covering and underlayment. If the underlayment is questionable or substandard, or if the floor covering is bonded to the underlayment, remove the flooring and underlayment together. Taking up both layers at once saves time.

Tips for Creating Sturdy Underlayment

Repair and prepare the subfloor. Before installing new underlayment and floor covering, fasten any sections of loose subfloor to floor joists, using deck screws. Fill in dips or gouges using leveling products.

Use quality materials. Using a quality underlayment that's appropriate for your floor covering is critical to the outcome of your flooring project. An inferior underlayment or improper installation will result in an imperfect surface when you're finished.

Tools for flooring removal and surface preparation include: a power sander (A), jamb saw (B), putty knife (C), floor roller (D), circular saw (E), hammer (F), hand maul (G), reciprocating saw (H), cordless drill (I), flat edged trowel (J), notched trowel (K), stapler (L), cat's paw (M), flat pry bar (N), heat gun (O), masonry chisel (P), crowbar (Q), nippers (R), wallboard knife (S), wood chisel (T), long-handled floor scraper (U), phillips screwdriver (V), standard screwdriver (W), utility knife (X), carpenter's level (Y).

Turn old flooring into a smooth underlayment layer for new flooring by applying an embossing leveler. Embossing leveler is a mortar-like substance that can prepare resilient flooring or ceramic tile, provided it's well adhered to the subfloor, for use as an underlayment for a new floor covering. Mix the leveler following manufacturer's directions, then spread it thinly over the floor, using a flat-edged trowel. Wipe away excess leveler with the trowel, making sure all dips and indentations are filled. Embossing leveler begins setting in 10 minutes, so work quickly. Once it dries, scrape away ridges and high spots with the trowel edge.

Installing Underlayment

Underlayment is a layer of sheeting that's screwed or nailed to the subfloor to provide a smooth, stable surface for the floor covering. The type of underlayment you choose depends in part on the type of floor covering you plan to install. For example, ceramic and natural stone tile floors usually require an underlayment that stands up to moisture, such as cementboard. For vinyl flooring, use a quality-grade plywood since most manufacturers' warranties are void if the flooring is installed over substandard underlayments. If you're using your old flooring as underlayment, apply an embossing leveler to prepare it for the new installation (see opposite page, bottom). Most wood flooring and carpeting do not require underlayment and are often placed directly on a plywood subfloor.

Plywood is the most common underlayment for vinyl flooring and some ceramic tile installations. For vinyl, use ¼" exterior-grade, AC plywood. This type has one smooth side for a quality surface. Wood-based floor coverings, like parquet, can be installed over lower-quality exterior-grade plywood. For ceramic tile, use ½" AC plywood. When installing plywood, leave ¼" expansion gaps at the walls and between sheets.

Fiber/cementboard is a thin, high-density underlayment used under ceramic tile and vinyl flooring in situations where floor height is a concern.

Cementboard is used only for ceramic tile or stone tile installations. It's stable even when wet and is therefore the best underlayment to use in areas likely to get wet, such as bathrooms. Cementboard is more expensive than plywood, but it's a good investment for a large tile installation.

Isolation membrane is used to protect ceramic tile installations from movement that may occur on cracked concrete floors. It's used primarily for covering individual cracks, but it can be used over an entire floor. Isolation membrane is also available in a liquid form that can be poured over the project area.

Plywood

Fiber/cement-board

Cementboard

Isolation membrane

Latex patching compound fills gaps, holes, and low spots in underlayment. It's also used to cover screw heads, nail heads, and seams in underlayment. Some compounds include dry and wet ingredients that need to be mixed, while others are premixed. The compound is applied with a trowel or wallboard knife.

How to Get Ready for a Flooring Project

Disconnect and remove all appliances. When bringing the appliances back into the room, protect your new floor by placing cardboard or a heavy cloth on the floor and in front of the appliance locations. Before setting the appliances in place, make sure the floor adhesives are properly cured.

Remove the toilet and other floor-mounted fixtures before installing a bathroom floor. Turn off and disconnect the water supply line, then remove the bolts holding the toilet on the floor.

Shovel old flooring debris out of your house through an open window and into a wheelbarrow. This helps speed up the demolition work. Protect plants and landscaping near the window with sheets of plywood.

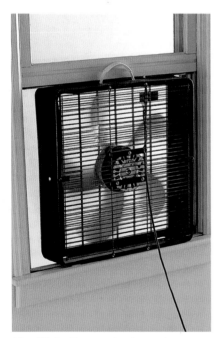

Ventilate the project room, especially when applying adhesives or removing old flooring. Placing a box fan in an open window will help draw dust and noxious fumes from the work area.

Cover entryways with sheet plastic to contain dust and debris while you remove the old floor.

Cover heat and air vents with sheet plastic and masking tape to prevent dust and debris from entering ductwork.

Removing Baseboards

Before removing your old floor covering, applying a new subfloor or underlayment, and installing a new floor, you'll need to remove your baseboards. Unless your floor covering is carpet, the baseboards sit on top of the floor to cover the gap between the floor and the wall.

If you're replacing carpet and will not be making any changes to the subfloor, you won't have to remove the baseboards, since the carpet butts up against them rather than going under them.

Use extreme care when removing the baseboards so you don't damage them. After you've replaced your floor, you'll need to replace your baseboards. Number the baseboards as you take them off the wall so you can put them back in the same order. When prying the boards loose, make sure to place a scrap piece of wood against the wall to avoid damaging the wall surface.

Tools & Materials:

Utility knife, pry bar, nippers, scrap wood.

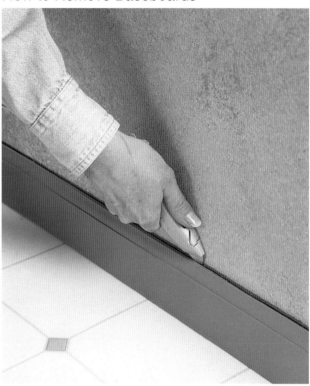

1 Cut the paint away from the baseboard with a utility knife.

2 Place a scrap board against the wall to avoid damaging the drywall. Remove the baseboard using a pry bar placed against the scrap board. Pry the baseboard at all nail locations. Number the baseboards as they are removed.

3 Remove the nails by pulling them through the back of the baseboard with nippers.

Use a floor scraper to remove resilient floor coverings and to scrape off leftover adhesives or backings. The long handle provides leverage and force, and it allows you to work in a comfortable standing position. A scraper will remove most of the flooring, but you may need other tools to finish the job.

Removing Floor Coverings

When old floor coverings must be removed, as is the case with many projects, thorough and careful removal work is essential to the quality of the new flooring installation.

The difficulty of flooring removal depends on the type of floor covering and the method that was used to install it. Carpet and perimeter-bond vinyl are generally very easy to remove, and removing vinyl tiles is also relatively simple. Full-spread sheet vinyl can be difficult to remove, however, and removing ceramic tile entails a lot of work.

With any removal project, be sure to keep your tool blades sharp, and avoid damaging the underlayment if you plan to reuse it. If you'll be replacing the underlayment, it may be easier to remove the old underlayment along with the floor covering.

Tools & Materials:

Floor scraper, utility knife, spray bottle, wallboard knife, wet/dry vacuum, heat gun, hand maul, masonry chisel, flat pry bar, end-cutting nippers, liquid dishwashing detergent.

How to Remove Sheet Vinyl

1 Use a utility knife to cut the old flooring into strips about a foot wide to make removal easier.

2 Pull up as much flooring as possible by hand. Grip the strips close to the floor to minimize tearing.

3 Cut stubborn sheet vinyl into strips about 6" wide. Starting at a wall, peel up as much of the floor covering as possible. If the felt backing remains, spray a solution of water and liquid dishwashing detergent under the surface layer to help separate the backing. Use a wallboard knife to scrape up particularly stubborn patches.

4 Scrape up the remaining sheet vinyl and backing with a floor scraper. If necessary, spray the backing with the soap solution to loosen it. Sweep up the debris, then finish the cleanup using a wet/dry vacuum. TIP: Fill the vacuum with about an inch of water to help contain dust.

How to Remove Vinyl Tiles

1 Starting at a loose seam, use a long-handled floor scraper to remove tiles. To remove stubborn tiles, soften the adhesive with a heat gun, then use a wallboard knife to pry up the tile and scrape off the underlying adhesive.

2 Remove stubborn adhesive or backing by wetting the floor with a mixture of water and liquid dishwashing detergent, then scrape it with a floor scraper.

How to Remove Ceramic Tile

1 Knock out tile using a hand maul and masonry chisel. If possible, start in a space between tiles where the grout has loosened. Be careful when working around fragile fixtures, such as drain flanges, so you don't damage them.

2 If you plan to reuse the underlayment, use a floor scraper to remove any remaining adhesive. You may have to use a belt sander with a coarse sanding belt to grind off stubborn adhesive.

How to Remove Carpet

1 Using a utility knife, cut around metal threshold strips to free the carpet. Remove the threshold strips with a flat pry bar.

2 Cut the carpet into pieces small enough to be easily removed. Roll up the carpet and remove it from the room, then remove the padding. NOTE: Padding is often stapled to the floor and usually comes up in pieces as you roll it.

3 Using end-cutting nippers or pliers, remove all of the staples from the floor. If you plan to lay new carpet, don't remove the tackless strips unless they're damaged.

Variation: To remove glued-down carpet, cut it into strips with a utility knife, then pull up as much material as you can. Scrape up the remaining cushion material and adhesive with a floor scraper.

Remove the underlayment and floor covering as though they're a single layer. This is an effective removal strategy with any floor covering that's bonded to the underlayment.

Removing Underlayment

Flooring contractors routinely remove the underlayment along with the floor covering before installing new flooring. This saves time and makes it possible to install new underlayment that's ideally suited to the new flooring. Do-it-yourselfers using this technique should make sure to cut the flooring into pieces that can be easily handled.

Warning: This floor removal method releases flooring particles into the air. Be sure the flooring you are removing does not contain asbestos.

Tools & Materials:
Goggles, gloves, circular saw with carbide-tipped blade, flat pry bar, reciprocating saw, wood chisel, hammer, protective ear and eye gear, dust mask.

Removal Tip

Examine fasteners to see how the underlayment is attached. Use a screwdriver to expose the heads of the fasteners. If the underlayment has been screwed down, you'll need to remove the floor covering and then unscrew the underlayment.

How to Remove Underlayment

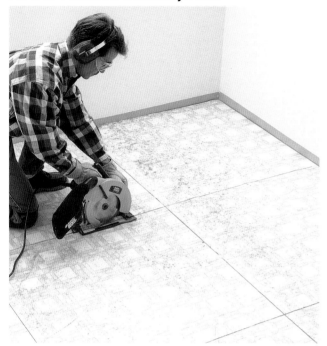

1 Adjust the cutting depth of a circular saw to equal the combined thickness of your floor covering and underlayment. Using a carbide-tipped blade, cut the floor covering and underlayment into squares measuring about 3 feet square. Be sure to wear safety goggles and gloves.

2 Use a reciprocating saw to extend the cuts to the edges of the walls. Hold the blade at a slight angle to the floor and be careful not to damage walls or cabinets. Don't cut deeper than the underlayment. Use a wood chisel to complete cuts near cabinets.

3 Separate the underlayment from the subfloor using a flat pry bar and hammer. Remove and discard the sections of underlayment and floor covering immediately, watching for exposed nails.

Variation: If your existing floor is ceramic tile over plywood underlayment, use a hand maul and masonry chisel to chip away the tile along the cutting lines before making cuts.

Repairing Subfloors

A solid, securely fastened subfloor minimizes floor movement and squeaks. It also ensures that your new floor covering will last a long time.

After removing the old underlayment, inspect the subfloor for loose seams, moisture damage, cracks, and other flaws. If your subfloor is made of dimension lumber rather than plywood, you can use plywood to patch damaged sections. If the plywood patch doesn't reach the height of the subfloor, use floor leveler to raise its surface to match the surrounding area.

Tools & Materials:

Finishing trowel, straightedge, framing square, drill, circular saw, cat's paw, wood chisel, hammer, tape measure, 2" deck screws, floor leveler, plywood, 2 × 4 lumber, 10d common nails, protective gloves.

Repair Tip

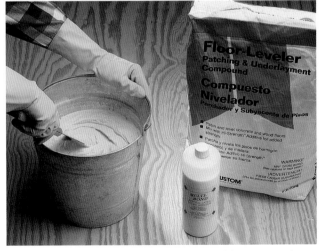

Floor leveler is used to fill in dips and low spots in plywood subfloors. Mix the leveler according to the manufacturer's directions, adding a latex or acrylic additive for added strength.

How to Apply Floor Leveler

1 Mix the leveler according to the manufacturer's directions, then spread it onto the subfloor using a finishing trowel. Build up the leveler in thin layers to avoid overfilling the area, allowing each layer to dry before applying the next.

2 Use a straightedge to make sure the filled area is level with the surrounding area. If necessary, apply more leveler. Allow the leveler to dry, then shave off any ridges with the edge of a trowel, or if necessary, sand it smooth.

How to Replace a Section of Subfloor

1 Use a framing square to mark a rectangle around the damage, making sure two sides of the rectangle are centered over floor joists. Remove nails along the lines, using a cat's paw. Make the cuts using a circular saw adjusted so the blade cuts through the subfloor only. Use a chisel to complete cuts near walls.

2 Remove the damaged section, then nail two 2 × 4 blocks between the joists, centered under the cut edges for added support. If possible, end-nail the blocks from below. Otherwise, toe-nail them from above, using 10d nails.

3 Measure the cut-out section, then cut a patch to fit. Use material that's the same thickness as the original subfloor. Fasten the patch to the joists and blocks using 2" deck screws spaced about 5" apart.

Repairing Joists

A severely arched, bulged, cracked, or sagging floor joist can only get worse over time, eventually deforming the floor above it. Correcting a problem joist is an easy repair and makes a big difference in your finished floor. It's best to identify problem joists and fix them before installing your underlayment and new floor covering.

One way to fix joist problems is to fasten a few new joists next to a damaged floor joist in a process called sistering. When installing a new joist, you may need to notch the bottom edge so it can fit over the foundation or beam. If that's the case with your joists, cut the notches in the ends no deeper than ⅛" of the actual depth of the joist. For example, a 2 × 12, which is actually 11½" wide, can have a notch 1⅞" deep.

Tools & Materials:

4-ft. level, reciprocating saw, hammer, chisel, adjustable wrench, tape measure, ratchet wrench, 3" lag screws with washers, framing lumber, 16d common nails, hardwood shims, metal jack posts.

How to Repair a Bulging Joist

1 Find the high point of the bulge in the floor using a level. Mark the high point and measure the distance to a reference point that extends through the floor, such as an exterior wall or heating duct.

2 Use the measurement and reference point from the last step to mark the high point on the joist from below the floor. From the bottom edge of the joist, make a straight cut into the joist just below the high point mark using a reciprocating saw. Make the cut ¾ of the depth of the joist. Allow several weeks for the joist to straighten.

3 When the joist has settled, reinforce it by centering a board of the same height and at least 6 ft. long next to it. Fasten the board to the joist by driving 12d common nails in staggered pairs about 12" apart. Drive a row of three nails on either side of the cut in the joist.

How to Repair a Cracked or Sagging Joist

1 Identify the cracked or sagging joist before it causes additional problems. Remove any blocking or bridging above the sill or beam where the sister joist will go.

2 Place a level on the bottom edge of the joist to determine the amount of sagging that has occurred. Cut a sister joist the same length as the damaged joist. Place it next to the damaged joist with the crown side up. If needed, notch the bottom edge of the sister joint so it fits over the foundation or beam.

3 Nail two 6-ft. 2 × 4s together to make a cross beam, then place the beam perpendicular to the joists near one end of the joists. Position a jack post under the beam and use a level to make sure it's plumb before raising it.

4 Raise the jack post by turning the threaded shaft until the cross beam is snug against the joists. Position a second jack post and cross beam at the other end of the joists. Raise the posts until the sister joist is flush with the subfloor. Insert tapered hardwood shims at the ends of the sister joist where it sits on the sill or beam. Tap the shims in place with a hammer and scrap piece of wood until they're snug.

5 Drill pairs of pilot holes in the sister joist every 12", then insert 3" lag screws with washers in each hole. Cut the blocking or bridging to fit and install it between the joists in its original position.

Installing Underlayment

When installing new underlayment, make sure it's securely attached to the subfloor in all areas, including under movable appliances. Notch the underlayment to fit the room's contours. Take the time to measure accurately and transfer the correct measurements onto your underlayment.

Rather than notching the underlayment around door casings, undercut moldings and door casings, then insert the underlayment beneath them.

For help in selecting the appropriate underlayment for your new flooring, refer to the guide on page 45.

Tools & Materials:

Drill, circular saw, wallboard knife, power sander, ¼" notched trowel, straightedge, utility knife, jig saw with carbide blade, ⅛" notched trowel, flooring roller, underlayment, 1" deck screws, floor-patching compound, latex additive, thin-set mortar, 1½" galvanized deck screws, fiberglass-mesh wallboard tape.

How to Install Plywood Underlayment

1 Install a full sheet of plywood along the longest wall, making sure the underlayment seams are not aligned with the subfloor seams. Fasten the plywood to the subfloor using 1" deck screws driven every 6" along the edges and at 8" intervals in the field of the sheet.

2 Continue fastening sheets of plywood to the subfloor, driving the screw heads slightly below the underlayment surface. Leave ¼" expansion gaps at the walls and between sheets. Offset seams in subsequent rows.

3 Using a circular saw or jig saw, notch the plywood to meet the existing flooring in doorways. Fasten the notched sheets to the subfloor.

4 Mix floor-patching compound and latex or acrylic additive following the manufacturer's directions. Spread it over seams and screw heads, using a wallboard knife.

5 Let the patching compound dry, then sand the patched areas, using a power sander.

How to Install Cementboard

1 Mix thin-set mortar according to the manufacturer's directions. Starting at the longest wall, spread the mortar on the subfloor in a figure-eight pattern using a ¼" notched trowel. Spread only enough mortar for one sheet at a time. Set the cementboard on the mortar with the rough side up, making sure the edges are offset from the subfloor seams.

2 Fasten the cementboard to the subfloor using 1¼" cementboard screws driven every 6" along the edges and 8" throughout the sheet. Drive the screw heads flush with the surface. Continue spreading mortar and installing sheets along the wall. OPTION: If installing fiber/cementboard underlayment, use a ⅜" notched trowel to spread the mortar, and drill pilot holes for all screws.

3 Cut cementboard pieces as necessary, leaving an ⅛" gap at all joints and a ¼" gap along the room perimeter. For straight cuts, use a utility knife to score a line through the fiber-mesh layer just beneath the surface, then snap the board along the scored line.

4 To cut holes, notches, or irregular shapes, use a jig saw with a carbide blade. Continue installing cementboard sheets to cover the entire floor.

5 Place fiberglass-mesh wallboard tape over the seams. Use a wallboard knife to apply thin-set mortar to the seams, filling the gaps between sheets and spreading a thin layer of mortar over the tape. Allow the mortar to set for two days before starting the tile installation.

How to Install Isolation Membrane

1 Thoroughly clean the subfloor, then apply thin-set mortar with a ⅛" notched trowel. Start spreading the mortar along a wall in a section as wide as the membrane and 8 to 10 ft. long. NOTE: For some membranes, you must use a bonding material other than mortar. Read and follow manufacturer's directions.

2 Roll out the membrane over the mortar. Cut the membrane to fit tightly against the walls, using a straightedge and utility knife.

3 Starting in the center of the membrane, use a heavy flooring roller to smooth out the surface toward the edges. This frees trapped air and presses out excess bonding material.

4 Repeat steps 1 through 3, cutting the membrane as necessary at the walls and obstacles, until the floor is completely covered with membrane. Do not overlap the seams, but make sure they're tight. Allow the mortar to set for two days before installing the tile.

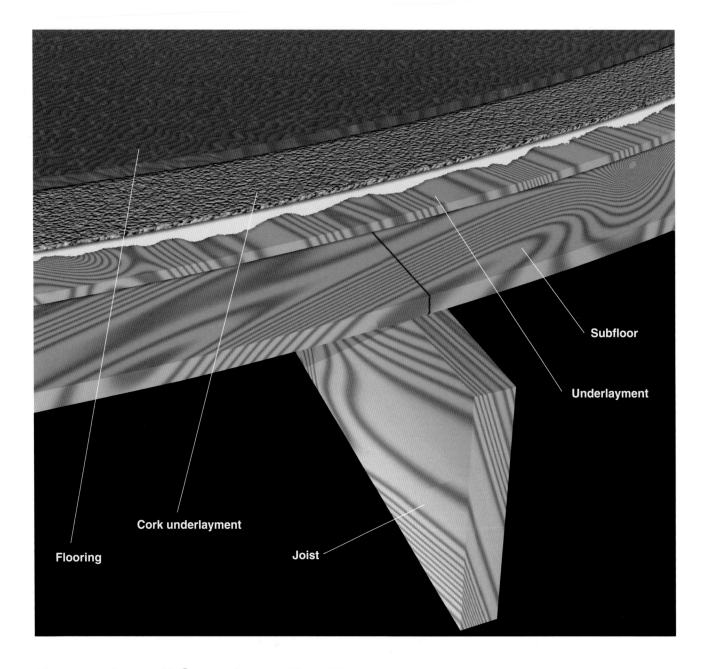

Subfloor

Underlayment

Cork underlayment

Joist

Flooring

How to Install Soundproofing Underlayment

Installing soundproofing underlayment will help eliminate noise in the floor and between rooms. It is primarily used under hard surface floor coverings, such as hardwood, ceramic tile, stone, and laminate.

There are a lot of different soundproofing materials on the market, including acoustic foam, recycled foam, and mineral wool. This project shows the installation of cork underlayment, which is a natural product that helps reduce noise.

Before installing the cork, place it in the room, making sure it's dry and well ventilated, for at least 72 hours prior to installation to allow it to

acclimate to the room. The cork is applied directly over a dry, level plywood underlayment placed over a plywood subfloor. The plywood underlayment has had all cracks, holes, and joints patched with cement-based compound. The floor covering is then placed directly over the cork.

Tools & Materials:

Utility knife, wallboard knife, v-notch trowel, straightedge, floor roller, cement-based compound, adhesive, cork underlayment.

How to Install Soundproofing Underlayment

1 Patch all holes, cracks, and joints in the plywood underlayment with cement-based compound, using a wallboard knife. The patches must be dry and the subfloor clean before continuing.

2 Cut the cork into 2" strips using a straightedge and utility knife. Using a manufacturer approved adhesive, apply the strips to the base of the walls so the bottom edge sits on the floor. Press firmly to eliminate air bubbles.

3 Unroll the cork the length of the room so the curled side is face down. Butt it against the 2" strips.

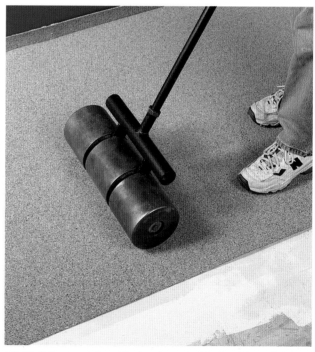

4 Pull back at least half of the roll. Apply adhesive to the plywood underlayment and spread it out, using a v-notch trowel. Replace the cork over the adhesive.

5 Roll the cork front to back and side to side using a floor roller. Repeat these steps to adhere the other half of the cork to the plywood underlayment. Cover the rest of the floor the same way. Butt joints tightly together, but don't overlap them.

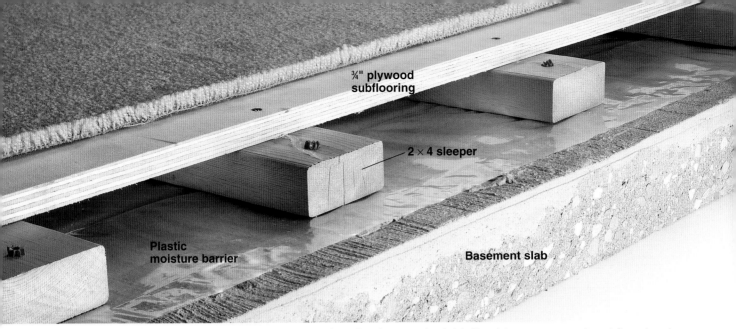

³⁄₄" plywood subflooring

2 × 4 sleeper

Plastic moisture barrier

Basement slab

Most basement floors need some preparation before flooring can be laid. Patching compound and floor leveler can smooth rough concrete, while a wood subfloor creates a new surface that feels like a framed wood floor.

Preparing Basement Floors

How you prepare a concrete basement floor largely depends on the condition of the floor, the floor covering you plan to use, and how you want the floor to feel underfoot. Floor manufacturers have specifications for installing their products over concrete. Follow these specs carefully since they may affect warranties. It's best to decide on a floor covering before preparing the floor. It's also imperative that you solve any moisture problems before covering a concrete floor.

To lay flooring directly over concrete, prepare the floor so it's smooth and flat. Fill cracks, holes, and expansion joints with a vinyl or cement-based floor-patching compound. If the concrete is especially rough or uneven, apply a floor leveler— a self-leveling, cement-based liquid that fills deviations in the floor and dries to form a hard, smooth surface.

For a more resilient basement floor, build a wood subfloor. A basement subfloor provides a flat, level surface that's more comfortable underfoot than concrete. It serves as a nailing surface for certain types of flooring. A subfloor does take up valuable headroom, so you may want to save space by using 1 × 4 sleepers instead of 2 × 4s. Consider how the added floor height will affect room transitions and the bottom step of the basement stairs.

Before laying out the sleepers, determine where the partition walls will go. If a wall will fall between parallel sleepers, add an extra sleeper to support the planned wall.

Tools & Materials:

Vacuum, masonry chisel, hammer, trowel, floor scraper, long-nap paint roller, wheelbarrow, utility knife, gage rake, 4-ft. level, circular saw, caulk gun, powder-actuated nailer, chalk line, drill, sledgehammer, vinyl floor-patching compound, concrete primer, floor leveler, pressure-treated 2 × 4s, 6-mil polyethylene sheeting, packing tape, cedar shims, construction adhesive, concrete fasteners, ³⁄₄" tongue-and-groove plywood, 2" wallboard screws.

Moisture Tip

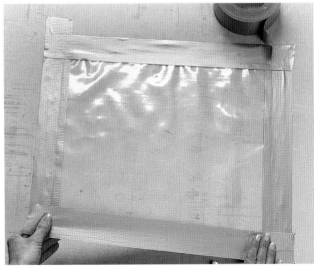

To test your floor for moisture, duct tape a 2 × 2 ft. piece of clear plastic to the concrete. Remove the plastic after 24 hours. If there's moisture on the plastic, you have a moisture problem. Do not install flooring until the problem has been fixed.

How to Patch Concrete Floors

1 Vacuum the floor and remove any loose or flaking concrete with a masonry chisel and hammer. Mix a batch of vinyl floor-patching compound, following the manufacturer's directions. Apply the compound using a smooth trowel, slightly overfilling the cavity. Smooth the patch flush with the surrounding surface.

2 After the compound has cured, use a floor scraper to scrape the patched areas smooth.

How to Apply Floor Leveler

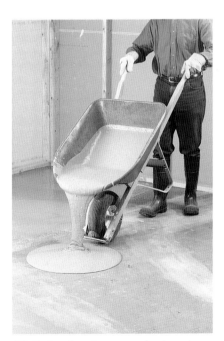

1 Remove any loose material and clean the concrete thoroughly so it's free of dust, dirt, oils, and paint. Apply an even layer of concrete primer to the entire surface using a long-nap paint roller. Let the primer dry completely before continuing.

2 Following the manufacturer's instructions, mix the floor leveler with water. The batch should be large enough to cover the entire floor area to the desired thickness (up to 1"). Pour the leveler over the floor.

3 Distribute the leveler evenly, using a gage rake or spreader. Work quickly since the leveler begins to harden in 15 minutes. Use a trowel to feather the edges and create smooth transitions with uncovered areas. Let the leveler dry for 24 hours.

How to Install a Basement Subfloor

1 Chip away loose or protruding concrete with a masonry chisel and hammer, then vacuum the floor. Roll out strips of 6-mil polyethylene sheeting, extending them 3" up each wall. Overlap strips by 6", then seal the seams with packing tape. Temporarily tape the edges along the walls. Be careful not to damage the sheeting.

2 Lay out pressure-treated 2 × 4s along the perimeter of the room. Position the boards ½" in from all walls (inset).

3 Using a circular saw, cut the sleepers to fit between the perimeter boards, leaving a ¼" gap at each end. Position the first sleeper so its center is 16" from the outside edge of the perimeter board. Lay out the remaining sleepers, using 16"-on-center spacing.

4 Where necessary, use tapered cedar shims to compensate for dips and variations in the floor. Place a 4-ft. level across neighboring sleepers. Apply construction adhesive to two wood shims. Slide the shims under the board from opposite sides until the board is level with adjacent sleepers.

5 Fasten the perimeter boards and sleepers to the floor using a powder-actuated nailer or masonry screws. Drive a fastener through the center of each board at 16" intervals. Fastener heads should not protrude above the board's surface. Place a fastener at each shim location, making sure the fastener penetrates both shims.

Control line

6 Establish a control line for the first row of plywood sheets by measuring 49" from the wall and marking the outside sleeper at each end of the room. Snap a chalk line across the sleepers at the marks. Run a ¼"-wide bead of adhesive along the first six sleepers, stopping just short of the control line.

7 Position the first sheet of plywood so the end is ½" away from the wall and the grooved edge is flush with the control line. Fasten the sheet to the sleepers using 2" wallboard screws. Drive a screw every 6" along the edges and every 8" in the field. Don't drive screws along the grooved edge until the next row of sheeting is in place.

Half-sheet

8 Install the remaining sheets in the first row, maintaining an ⅛" gap between ends. Begin the second row with a half-sheet (4 ft. long) so the end joints between rows are staggered. Fit the tongue of the half sheet into the groove of the adjoining sheet. If necessary, use a sledgehammer and wood block to help close the joint (inset). After completing the second row, begin the third row with a full sheet. Alternate this pattern until the subfloor is complete.

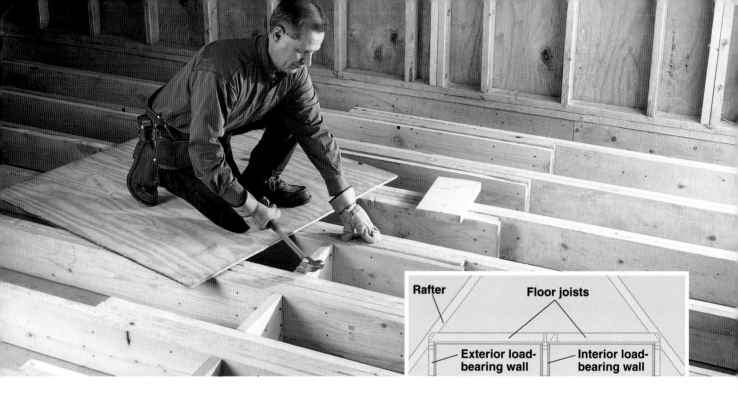

Rafter   Floor joists

Exterior load-bearing wall   Interior load-bearing wall

Building Attic Floors

Existing floors in most unfinished attics are merely ceiling joists and are too small to support living spaces. However, if your floor already has floor trusses, joists 2 × 8 or larger, or the same framing as the floor on your main level, it probably doesn't need additional framing. If you're unsure, consult a professional.

There are several options for strengthening your attic's floor structure. The simplest method is to install an additional, identically sized joist next to each existing joist and nail the two together. This process, known as sistering, is done when the current joists are damaged or loose, squeak, or can't support additional weight.

Sistering doesn't work when joists are smaller than 2 × 6, where joists are spaced too far apart, or where there are obstructions, such as plaster keys from the ceiling below. An alternative is to build a new floor by placing larger joists between the existing ones. By resting the joists on 2 × 4 spacers, you avoid obstructions and minimize damage to the ceiling surfaces below. Be aware that the spacers will reduce your headroom by 1½" in addition to the depth of the joists.

To determine the best flooring option for your attic, consult an architect, engineer, or general contractor as well as a local building inspector. Ask what size joists you'll need and which options the building codes in your area allow. Joist sizing is based on the span (the distance between support points), the joist spacing (typically 16" or 24"

on center), and the type of lumber used. In most cases, an attic floor must be able to support 40 pounds per square feet (psf) of live load, such as occupants and furniture, and 10 psf of dead load, including wallboard and floor covering.

Floor joist cavities offer space for concealing the plumbing, wiring, and ductwork servicing your attic, so consider these systems as you plan. Plan the locations of partition walls to determine if additional blocking between joists is necessary.

When the framing is done, the mechanical elements and insulation are in place, and everything has been inspected and approved, complete the floor by installing ¾" tongue-and-groove (T&G) plywood. If your remodel will include kneewalls, you can omit the subflooring behind the knee-walls, but there are good reasons not to. A complete subfloor adds strength and provides a sturdy surface for storage. Before starting the project, check with your local building department to see if you need to procure a building permit.

Tools & Materials:

Circular saw, rafter square, drill, tape measure, caulk gun, joist lumber, 16d common nails, 10d common nails, 8d common nails, 2 × 4 lumber, ¾" tongue-&-groove plywood, construction adhesive, 2¼" wallboard screws.

How to Add Sister Joists

1 Remove all insulation from the joist cavities and carefully remove any blocking or bridging between the joists. Determine the lengths for the sister joists by measuring the existing joists. Also measure the outside end of each joist to determine how much of the top corner needs to be cut away to fit the joist beneath the roof sheathing. NOTE: Joists that rest on a bearing wall should overlap each other by at least 3".

2 Before cutting the joists, sight down both narrow edges of each board to check for crowning, which is an upward arching along the length of the board. Draw an arrow pointing toward the arch. Joists must be installed crown side up. Cut the board to length, then clip the top outside corner to match the existing joist.

3 Set the sister joists in place, flush against the existing joists with their ends aligned. Toenail each sister joist to the top plates of both supporting walls using two 16d common nails.

4 Facenail the joists together using 10d common nails. Drive three nails in a row, spacing the rows 12" to 16" apart. To minimize damage (such as cracking and nail popping) to the ceiling surface below, you can use a pneumatic nail gun or 3" lag screws instead of nails. Install new blocking between the sistered joists as required by the local building code.

How to Build an Attic Floor Using New Joists

1 Remove any blocking or bridging from between the existing joists, being careful not to disturb the ceiling below. Cut 2 × 4 spacers to fit snugly between each pair of joists. Lay the spacers flat on the top plate of each supporting wall. Nail the spacers to the top plates using 16d common nails.

2 Create a layout for the new joists by measuring across the tops of existing joists and using a rafter square to transfer the measurements down to the spacers. Using 16"-on-center spacing, mark the layout along one exterior wall, then mark an identical layout on the interior bearing wall. The layout on the opposing exterior wall will be offset 1½" to account for the joist overlap at the interior wall.

3 Measure from the outer edge of the exterior wall to the far edge of the interior bearing wall. The joists must overlap above the interior wall by at least 3". Measure the outside end of each joist to determine how much of the top corner needs to be cut away to fit under the roof sheathing. Cut the joists to length, then clip the top outside corners as necessary.

4 Set the joists in place on their layout marks. Toenail the outside end of each joist to the spacer on the exterior wall using three 8d common nails.

5 Nail the joists together where they overlap atop the interior bearing wall, using three 10d common nails for each connection. Toenail the joists to the spacers on the interior bearing wall, using 8d common nails.

6 Install blocking or bridging between the joists, as required by your local building code. As a suggested minimum, the new joists should be blocked as close as possible to the outside ends and at the points where they overlap at the interior wall.

How to Install Subflooring

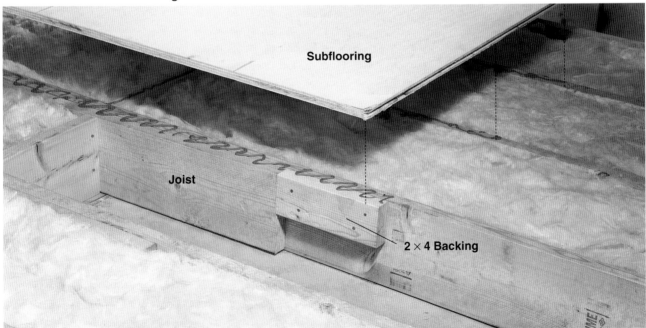

Subflooring

Joist

2 × 4 Backing

Install the subfloor only after all of the framing, plumbing, wiring, and ductwork are complete and have passed the necessary building inspections. Install insulation as needed and complete any caulking necessary for soundproofing. Fasten the subflooring sheets with construction adhesive and 2¼" wallboard or deck screws, making sure the sheets are perpendicular to the joists and the end joints are staggered between rows. Where joists overlap at an interior bearing wall, add backing as needed to compensate for the offset in the layout. Nail a 2 × 4 (or wider) board to the face of each joist to support the edges of the sheets.

Installing a Floor-warming System

Ceramic tile is a great floor covering, but it has a significant drawback: It's cold on bare feet. An easy way to remedy this is to install a floor-warming system.

A typical floor-warming system consists of thin mats containing electric resistance wires that heat up when energized, like an electric blanket. The mats are installed under the floor covering and hard-wired to a 120-volt GFCI circuit. A thermostat controls the floor temperature and a timer turns the system on and off automatically. The systems require very little energy and are designed to heat only the floor. They're not used as a room's sole heat source.

A crucial part of installing this system is to perform several resistance checks to ensure the heating wires have not been damaged. The electrical service required for a floor-warming system is based on its size. If you're installing a new circuit, consider hiring an electrician to make the connection at the service panel.

To order a floor-warming system, contact a manufacturer or dealer. In most cases, you can send in floor plans and the manufacturer will custom-fit a system for your project. The systems can also be used under laminate, vinyl, and floating floors. Don't use them under a wood covering that requires nailing, since the nails can puncture the electric wires. Also, don't use asphalt felt paper as an underlayment. When the paper warms up, it can smell very unpleasant. Use rosen paper rather than felt paper.

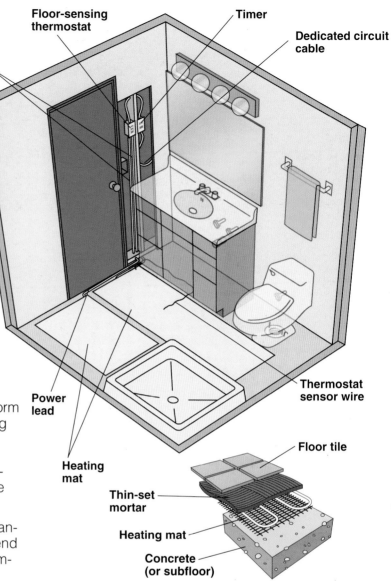

Floor-warming systems must be installed on a circuit with adequate amperage and a GFCI breaker (some systems have built-in GFCIs). Smaller systems may tie into an existing circuit, but larger ones often need a dedicated circuit. Follow all local building and electrical codes that apply to your project.

Tools & Materials:

Multi-tester, drill, plumb bob, chisel, tubing cutter, combination tool, vacuum, chalk line, grinder, glue gun, fish tape, aviation snips, ⅜ × ¼" square-notched trowel, tile tools and materials, floor-warming system, 2½ × 4" double-gang electrical box with 4" adapter cover, 2½"-deep single-gang electrical box, ½"-dia. thin-wall conduit, setscrew fittings, 12-gauge NM cable, cable clamps, double-sided tape, electrical tape, insulated cable clamps, wire connectors.

How to Install a Floor-warming System

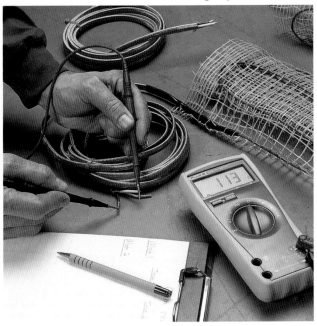

1 Check the resistance value (ohm) of each heating mat using a digital multi-tester. Record the reading. Compare your reading to the factory-tested reading noted by the manufacturer. Your reading must fall within the acceptable range determined by the manufacturer. If it doesn't, the mat has been damaged and should not be installed. Contact the manufacturer for assistance.

2 Remove the wall surface to expose the framing. Locate the electrical boxes approximately 60" from the floor, making sure the power leads on the heating mats will reach the electrical box. Mount a 2½"-deep × 4"-wide double-gang electrical box for the thermostat to the wall stud. Mount a single-gang electrical box for the timer on the other side of the stud.

3 Use a plumb bob or level to mark points on the bottom wall plate directly below the two knockouts on the thermostat box. At each mark, drill a ½" hole through the top of the plate. Drill two more holes as close as possible to the floor through the side of the plate, intersecting the top holes. Clean up the holes with a chisel to ensure smooth routing.

4 Cut two lengths of ½" thin-wall electrical conduit with a tubing cutter to fit between the thermostat box and the bottom plate. Place the bottom end of each conduit about ¼" into the respective holes in the bottom plate and fasten the top ends to the thermostat box using setscrew fittings. If you're installing three or more mats, use ¾" conduit instead of ½".

Setscrew fittings

(continued next page)

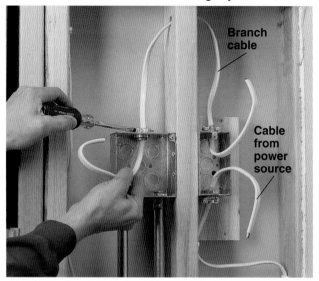

Branch cable

Cable from power source

5 Run 12-gauge NM electrical cable from the service panel (power source) to the timer box. Attach the cable to the box with a cable clamp, leaving 8" of extra cable extending into the box. Drill a ⅝" hole through the center of the stud about 12" above the boxes. Run a short branch cable from the timer box to the thermostat box, securing both ends with clamps. The branch cable should make a smooth curve where it passes through the stud.

2" minimum

6 Vacuum the floor thoroughly. Plan the ceramic tile layout and snap reference lines for the tile installation (see page 80). Spread the heating mats over the floor so the power leads are close to the electrical boxes. Position the mats 3" to 6" away from walls, showers, bathtubs, and toilet flanges. Place the mats in the kick space of a vanity, but not under the vanity cabinet or over expansion joints in the concrete slab. Set the edges of the mats close together, but don't overlap them. The heating wires in one mat must be at least 2" away from the wires in the neighboring mat.

7 Confirm that the power leads still reach the thermostat box. Secure the mats to the floor using strips of double-sided tape spaced every 2 ft. Make sure the mats are lying flat with no wrinkles or ripples. Press firmly to secure the mats to the tape.

8 Create recesses in the floor for the connections between power leads and heating-mat wires, using a grinder or a cold chisel and hammer. These insulated connections are too thick to lay under the tile and must be recessed to within ⅛" of the floor. Clean away any debris and secure the connections in the recesses with a bead of hot glue.

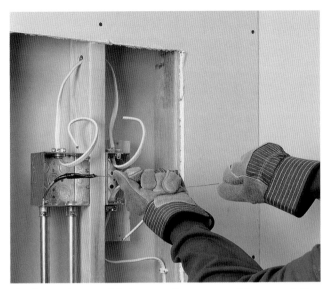

9 Thread a steel fish tape down one of the conduits and attach the ends of the power leads to the fish tape using electrical tape. Pull the fish tape and leads up through the conduit. Disconnect the fish tape, then secure the leads to the box with insulated cable clamps. Use aviation snips or linesman's pliers to cut off excess from the leads, leaving 8" extending past the clamps.

10 Feed the heat sensor wire through the remaining conduit and weave it into the mesh of the nearest mat. Use dabs of hot glue to secure the sensor wire directly between two blue resistance wires, extending it 6" to 12" into the mat. Test the resistance of the heating mats with a multi-tester as you did in step 1 to make sure the resistance wires have not been damaged. Record the reading.

11 Install the floor tile as shown on pages 150 to 157. Using thin-set mortar as an adhesive, spread it carefully over the floor and mats with a ⅜ × ¼" square-notched trowel. Check the resistance of the mats periodically as you install the tile. If a mat becomes damaged, clean up any exposed mortar and contact the manufacturer. When the installation is complete, check the resistance of the mats once again and record the reading.

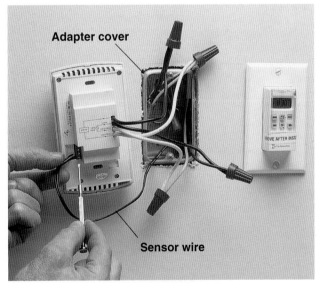

Adapter cover

Sensor wire

12 Install an adapter cover (mud ring) to the thermostat box, then patch the wall opening with wallboard. Complete the wiring connections for the thermostat and timer following the manufacturer's instructions. Attach the sensor wire to the thermostat setscrew connection. Apply the manufacturer's wiring labels to the thermostat box and service panel. Mount the thermostat and timer. Complete the circuit connection at the service panel or branch connection. After the flooring materials have cured, test the system.

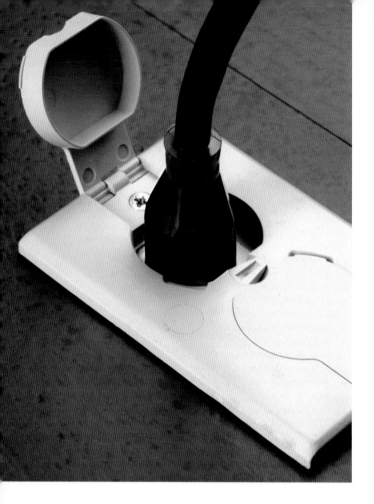

Installing an In-floor Electrical Outlet

Installing an electrical outlet in the floor is surprisingly simple. Floor box kits have everything you need to add an outlet in any room. The outlet is covered when not in use to protect against debris falling into the receptacle.

The outlet is placed in the subfloor before the floor covering is installed. If the floor is already finished, remove an area of flooring.

Before installing an outlet, check with your local building department for any restrictions.

Tools & Materials:

Floor box assembly kit, screwdriver, cordless drill, jig saw.

How to Install an In-floor Electrical Outlet

1 Place the box on the subfloor where the outlet will be installed. Make sure it's next to a floor joist. Trace around the box. Remove the box, then drill holes at the corners on the floor. Cut out the opening, using a jig saw.

2 Place the clip for the floor box in the opening so the lip sits on top of the subfloor. Attach the clip to the subfloor and joist using the four 1¼" self-tapping screws that came with the kit.

3 Slide the box onto the clip so the adjusting screw is aligned with the threads on the clip. Screw the box into the clip, lowering the box into place. Do not set the box all the way to the subfloor.

4 Turn off the power at the main power source. Insert electrical wires into the box and wire the receptacle in accordance with your local building codes. Push the wires and receptacle inside the box.

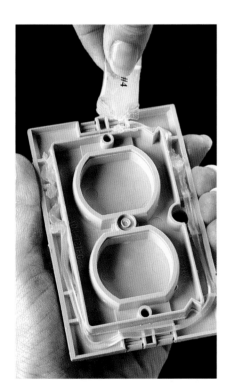

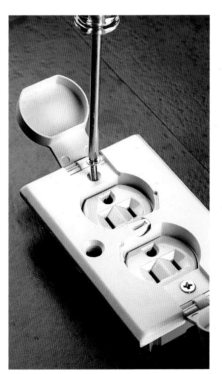

5 Install the floor covering. Using the sealant that came with the kit, apply a ⅛"-thick bead of sealant around the outside rib of the cover where it fits over the box.

6 With the outlet caps open, set the cover on the box. Align the holes with the recessed bosses and the "button" hole with the adjustable screw. Insert two machine screws and tighten, but don't overtighten.

7 Turn the adjustable screw to set the face of the outlet at the desired height. Place the button that came with the kit in the button hole.

Cutting Door Casing

Unless you're installing carpet, you'll want your floor covering to fit under your door casing. This allows the casing to cover the gap between the flooring and the wall, and it allows wood floors to expand and contract without dislodging the casing. If you try to butt your flooring against your casing, you'll end up with an unsightly gap.

It only takes a few minutes to cut the casing. If you're installing ceramic tile or parquet, keep in mind you'll be placing the flooring over adhesive, so cut the casing about an ⅛" above the top of tile to allow for the height of the adhesive.

These directions show the casing being cut to accommodate ceramic tile. Because the tile will be placed on top of cementboard, a piece of cementboard is placed under the tile when the casing is marked.

Cut the bottom of door casings the thickness of your flooring and underlayment so your floor covering will fit under it.

Tools & Materials:

Jamb saw, floor covering.

How to Cut Door Casing

1 Place a piece of flooring and underlayment against the door casing. Mark the casing about an ⅛" above the top of the flooring.

2 Cut the casing at the mark using a jamb saw.

3 Slide a piece of flooring under the door jamb to make sure it fits easily.

Measuring Your Room

You'll need to determine the total square footage of your room before ordering your floor covering. To do this, divide the room into a series of squares and rectangles that you can easily measure. Be sure to include all areas that will be covered, such as closets and space under your refrigerator and other movable appliances.

Measure the length and width of each area in inches, then multiply the length times the width. Divide that number by 144 to determine your square footage. Add all of the areas together to figure the square footage for the entire room, then subtract the areas that will not be covered, such as cabinets and other permanent fixtures.

When ordering your floor covering, be sure to purchase 10 to 15% extra to allow for waste and cutting. For patterned flooring, you may need as much as 20% extra.

Measure the area of the project room to calculate how much flooring you will need.

How to Measure Your Room

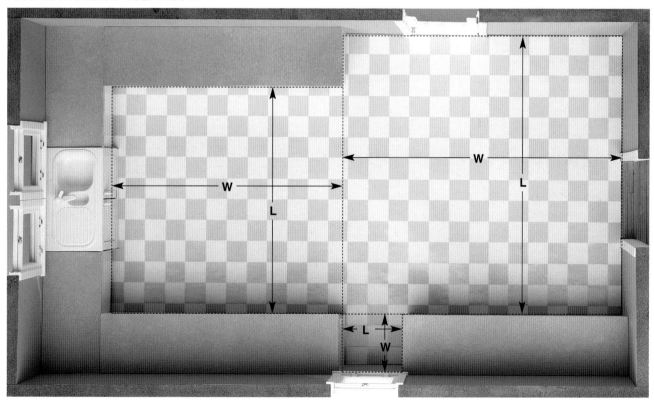

Divide the room into rectangles or squares. Include closets and areas where moveable appliances are installed. Measure the length and width of each area in inches, then multiply the length times the width. Divide that number by 144 to determine your square footage.

To check your reference lines for squareness, use the 3-4-5 triangle method. Measuring from your centerpoint, make a mark along a reference line at 3 ft. and along a perpendicular reference line at 4 ft. The distance between the two points should be exactly 5 ft. If it's not, adjust your lines accordingly.

Establishing Reference Lines

Your first row of flooring, your first few tiles, or your first piece of sheeting sets the direction for the rest of your floor. It's critical, therefore, to get off to a perfect start. You can do this by carefully planning your layout and establishing accurate reference lines.

In general, tile flooring begins at the center of the room and is installed in quadrants along layout lines, also called working lines. After establishing reference lines that mark the center of the room, lay the tile in a dry run along those lines to ensure you won't have to cut off more than half of a tile in the last row. If necessary, adjust your reference lines by half the width of the tile to form your layout lines.

For most floating floors and tongue-and-groove

floors, you only need a single reference line along the starting wall. If your wall is straight, you don't even need a working line. You can place spacers along the wall and butt the first row of flooring against the spacers. However, this only works if your wall is straight. If it's bowed or out of square, it will affect your layout.

The photos on the next page show the options for establishing reference lines to get started with your floor installation.

Tools & Materials:

Tape measure, chalk line, framing square, hammer, 8d finish nails, spacers.

How to Establish Reference Lines for Tile

Mark the centerpoint of opposite walls, then snap a chalk line between the marks. Mark the centerpoint of the chalk line. Place a framing square at the centerpoint so one side is flush with the chalk line. Snap a perpendicular reference along the adjacent side of the framing square (see page 135).

Snap chalk lines between the centerpoints of opposite walls to establish perpendicular reference lines. Check the lines for squareness using the 3-4-5 triangle method (see page 80).

How to Establish Reference Lines for Wood and Floating Floors

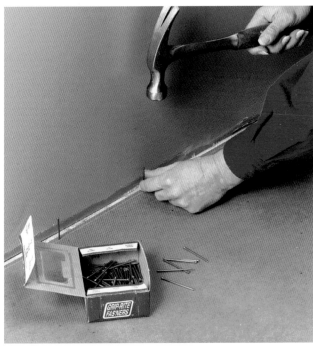

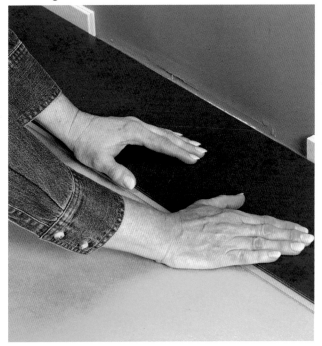

If your wall is out of square or bowed, make a mark on the floor ½" from the wall at both ends and snap a chalk line. Drive 8d finish nails every 2" to 3" along the line. Use this as your reference line and butt the first row of flooring against the nails (see page 94).

If your wall is straight, place ½" spacers along the wall, then butt your flooring up against the spacers (see page 118).

Hardwood Floor Coverings

Hardwood is a traditional favorite for floors. It adds character and sets the mood for a room. The classic beauty of hardwood lends itself to any decorating style and trend while providing a consistent element for tying rooms together.

Although hardwood was once reserved for formal rooms, it's now used in virtually every room in the home, including kitchens. Unlike other floor coverings, hardwood will last a lifetime. If properly maintained, it can actually look more charming as it ages.

As you'll see in this section, there are a variety of wood floor coverings that require different installation techniques. Tongue-and-groove strip flooring is installed using a power nailer; parquet and end grain floors are set in adhesive, while floating floors fasten together at the tongue-and-groove connections and are not connected to the floor at all.

Wood floors absorb moisture from the humidity in the air, causing the wood to expand. When the air is dry, wood contracts. The flooring is kept ½" from the walls to allow for this expansion and contraction. The gap is covered by the baseboard and base shoe.

Wood must be "acclimated" to the room in which it will be installed. Place the flooring in the room under normal temperatures and humidity conditions. The length of this acclimation period varies, sometimes taking up to a full week, so check manufacturer's recommendations before installing.

Photos this page courtesy of MIRAGE Prefinished Hardwood Floors

Hardwood Flooring Options

Hardwood flooring has undeniable appeal, but installing traditional solid hardwood strips or planks has intimidated many do-it-yourselfers. Solid hardwood flooring is typically more expensive than other floor coverings, and installation can be time consuming. Nevertheless, it's still a project you can do yourself by following the instructions on pages 94 to 96.

There are other hardwood flooring products available that were designed for do-it-yourself installation. These materials offer the virtues of solid hardwood, such as strength, durability, attractiveness, and warm appearance, but they're easier to install.

These composite products come already stained and sealed with a protective coating. Like their solid hardwood counterparts, manufactured flooring features tongue-and-groove construction that ensures a tight bond between pieces.

Laminated planks can be installed one of two ways. They can be installed on a thin layer of adhesive, which is a good choice for areas that get a lot of foot traffic. They can also be installed as a floating floor, which rests on a thin padding and can be installed over a variety of surfaces. Floating floors are the ideal choice for installation over concrete slabs (see pages 118 to 121).

Parquet flooring is installed with flooring adhesive, using techniques similar to ceramic tile installation. Parquet is a good choice for formal rooms or where you want a decorative pattern (see pages 104 to 107).

Hardwood Flooring Options

Fiberboard

Plywood

Parquet

Manufactured wood flooring materials include: fiberboard surfaced with a synthetic laminate layer that mimics the look of wood grain (left), plywood topped with a thin hardwood veneer (center), and a parquet tile made of wood strips bonded together in a decorative pattern (right).

Solid hardwood flooring is more expensive and more difficult to install than manufactured wood flooring.

Stripping and refinishing an existing solid hardwood floor will give you a surface that looks like new. See the Floor Finishes section beginning on page 198.

Power tools for hardwood flooring installation include: miter saw (A), circular saw (B), jig saw (C), rubber mallet (D), power nailer (E), cordless drill (F).

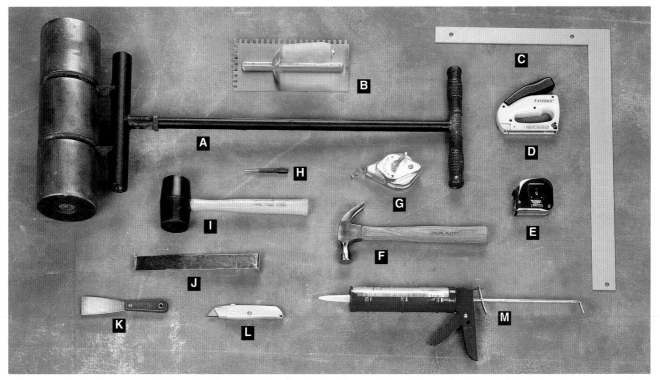

Hand tools for hardwood flooring installation include: floor roller (A), notched trowel (B), framing square (C), stapler (D), tape measure (E), hammer (F), chalk line (G), nail set (H), rubber mallet (I), floor pull bar (J), putty knife (K), utility knife (L), caulk gun (M).

How to Cut Hardwood Flooring

Ripcut hardwood planks from the back side to avoid splintering the top surface. Measure the distance from the wall to the edge of the last board installed, subtracting ½" to allow for an expansion gap. Transfer the measurement to the back of the flooring, and mark the cut with a chalk line.

When ripcutting hardwood flooring with a circular saw, place another piece of flooring next to the one marked for cutting to provide a stable surface for the foot of the saw. Clamp a cutting guide to the planks to ensure a straight cut.

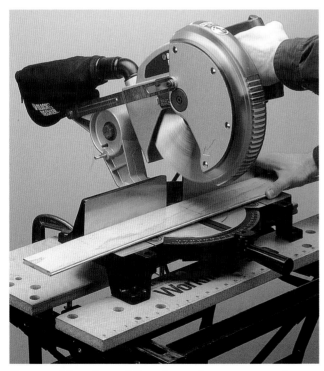

Crosscut hardwood flooring using a power miter box. Place the top surface face up to prevent splintering.

Make notched or curved cuts in hardwood flooring with a coping saw or jig saw. If using a jig saw, the finished surface should face down. Clamp the flooring to your work surface when cutting.

Filling in the Gaps

When you install wood or laminate floors, leave a ½" gap between the perimeter of the floor and the walls to allow the wood to expand and contract with changes in temperature and humidity.

You will also have gaps that need to be covered at thresholds, between rooms, and around small obstacles, such as pipes. For every situation, there is a molding to fit your needs.

A floor isn't truly finished until all of the pieces are in place. These moldings help give your floors a professional look. The names for moldings may differ slightly between manufacturers.

Wood molding is used for a smooth transition between the hardwood in the dining area and the tile in the adjoining room.

T-moldings span transitions between hardwood floors and other floors of equal height. These products are usually glued in place.

Reducer strips provide a transition between a wood floor and an adjacent floor of a lower height. One edge is grooved to fit the tongue in the hardwood.

A. Carpet reducers are used to finish off and create a smooth transition between flooring and carpeting.

B. Stair nosing is used to cover the exposed edges of stairs where the risers meet the steps. It is also used between step-downs and landings.

C. Baby threshold is used in place of baseboards and quarter round in front of sliding glass doors or door thresholds, to fill the gap between the floor and door.

D. Reducer strips, also called transition strips, are used between rooms when the floors are at different heights and composed of different materials.

E. Overlap reducers are also used between rooms when one floor is at a different height than an adjoining room.

F. T-moldings are used to connect two floors of equal height. They are also used in doorways and thresholds to provide a smooth transition. T-moldings do not butt up against the flooring, allowing the wood to expand and contract under it.

G. Baseboards are used for almost all types of floors and are available in a wide variety of designs and thicknesses. They are applied at the bottom of walls to cover the gap between the floor and walls.

H. Quarter round, similar to shoemolding, is installed along the bottom edge of base board and sits on top of the floor. It covers any remaining gaps between the floor and walls.

Installing Tongue-and-Groove Hardwood Flooring

Tongue-and-groove hardwood flooring has always been popular with homeowners. It offers an attractive look, is one of the longest lasting floor coverings, and can be stripped and refinished to look like new.

Oak has been the most common type of strip flooring because of its durability and wood graining, and it's the species most people think of when "hardwood" is mentioned. Other woods, such as maple, cherry, and birch, are also becoming popular.

Exotic species of wood from around the world are now finding their way into American homes as people want a premium strip or plank floor that's unique and stylish, and expresses their personalities. The more than 60 exotic hardwoods include Brazilian cherry, Australian cypress, Honduran mahogany, tobaccowood, teak, zebrawood, and bamboo.

This section describes how to install nailed-down tongue-and-groove bamboo flooring (pages 94 to 96), how to install a decorative medallion (page 97), and how to install tongue-and-groove strip flooring over troweled-on adhesive (pages 98 to 99). Customizing your floor with borders, accents, and medallions is easier than you think. A number of manufacturers produce a variety of decorative options made to match the thickness of your floor.

The shine on this hardwood plank floor catches the eye of everyone who enters the room. The dark color of the flooring matches the wicker furniture and the wooden stairs.

The key to a good tongue-and-groove floor is a good subfloor. A solid subfloor free of imperfections will help prevent squeaks and movement in the wood flooring. Here are recommendations for installing tongue-and-groove flooring over existing floors:

Resilient Floors: When covering a resilient floor, glue down any loose tiles or corners and fill in any low spots.

Old Wood Floors: When covering an old wood floor, nail down any loose boards, replace warped or cupped boards that won't lay flat, and set raised nails. Run new floor boards in a different direction than current boards by installing them diagonally or perpendicular to the existing

floor. If you want to run the floor in the same direction, overlay the floor with ⅜" or ½" plywood first. Keep in mind that this will raise your floor height and that you may have to trim the bottoms off doors so they can swing freely.

Ceramic tiles: When covering a ceramic tile floor, remove all tiles and overlay the subfloor with ⅝" plywood.

Concrete: When covering concrete, make sure a proper subfloor is in place and the floor is at or above grade. Make sure moisture is not a problem. New concrete typically has a lot of moisture and should not be used under a wood floor.

Installing tongue-and-groove strips or planks is

The decorative border in the hardwood floor on the left provides an ideal accent to match the wall covering. The beech wood in the above floor captures the essence of natural wood. Walnut is the perfect choice for the floor below to contrast with the light-colored walls.

straightforward. The first and last boards are face nailed, while the other boards are blind nailed. Once the first few rows are installed, you can use a power nailer. This lets you install floor boards without pre-drilling holes and setting nails, greatly reducing your installation time. Be sure to measure and cut boards at the appropriate ends to ensure tongue-and-groove joints fit together for "end matches."

To protect your hardwood, don't drag furniture over the floor. Place protective rests under furniture that sits on the floor. Direct sunlight can fade the gloss on hardwood, so keep the shades drawn as needed. Some footwear can also damage hardwood, especially narrow-heeled shoes.

Tools & Materials:

Miter saw, circular saw, stapler, utility knife, tape measure, chalk line, drill, flooring pull bar, rubber mallet, hammer, pry bar, power nailer, rosin paper, wood floor strips or planks, nails or staples, reducer strip or transition strip, wood putty. If installing the floor using adhesive, you'll also need: coping saw, ⅛" notched trowel, floor roller, flooring adhesive, wood glue, cardboard.

How to Install Tongue-and-Groove Flooring

1 Cover the entire subfloor with rosin paper. Staple the paper to the subfloor, overlapping edges by 4". Cut the paper with a utility knife to butt against the walls.

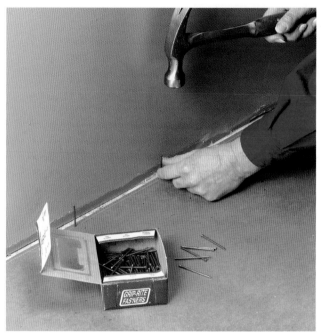

2 Make a mark on the floor ½" from the starter wall at both ends of the wall. Snap a chalk line between the marks. Nail 8d finish nails every 2" to 3" along the chalk line to mark the location for your first row.

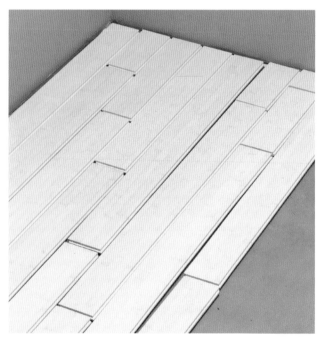

3 Lay out the first 8 rows of flooring in a dry run with the groove side facing the wall. Make sure the first row of boards is straight. Arrange the boards to get a good color and grain mix. Offset the ends by at least 6".

4 Place the starter row against the nails on the chalk line. Drill pilot holes in the flooring every 6" to 8", about ½" from the groove edge. Face nail the first row until the nail heads are just above the boards, then sink them using a nail set. (Be careful not to hit the boards with your hammer or you'll mar the surface.)

5 Drill pilot holes every 6" to 8" directly above the tongue, keeping the drill at a 45° angle.

Tip: To install crooked boards, drill pilot holes above the tongue and insert nails. Fasten a scrap board to the subfloor using screws. Force the floor board straight using a pry bar and a scrap board placed in front of the flooring. With pressure on the floor board, blind nail it into place.

6 Blind nail a nail into each pilot hole. Keep the nail heads ½" out, then set them just below the surface, using a nail set.

7 Set the second row of boards in place against the starter row, fitting together the tongue and groove connections. Use a scrap board and rubber mallet to tap the floor boards together. Drill pilot holes and blind nail the boards. Do this for the next few rows.

8 To install the last board in a row, place the tongue and groove joints together, then place a flooring pull bar over the end of the board. Hit the end of the pull bar with a hammer until the board slides into place. Stay ½" away from the walls.

(continued next page)

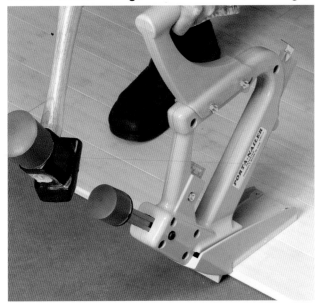

9 Once you have several rows installed and have enough room, use a power nailer. Place the nailer lip over the edge of the board and strike it with a rubber mallet. Drive a nail 2" from the end of each board and about every 8" in the field. Keep a few rows of flooring laid out ahead of you as you work, and keep the joints staggered.

10 When you're out of room for the power nailer, drill pilot holes and blind nail the boards. For the last rows, drill pilot holes in the top of the boards, ½" from the tongue, and face nail them. The last row may need to be ripped to size. Pull the last row into place using the flooring pull bar, leaving a ½" gap along the wall. Drill pilot holes and face nail.

11 Install a reducer strip or transition strip between the wood floor and an adjoining room. Cut the strip to size. Fit the strip's groove over the floor board's tongue, then drill pilot holes and face nail. Set the nails with a nail set. Fill all visible nail holes with wood putty.

Tip: To install around an object, cut a notch in the board. For larger obstacles, cut 45° miters in boards so the grooves face away from the object. Rip the tongues off the boards. Set the boards against the object and the flooring, fitting the mitered ends together. Drill pilot holes and face nail in place. Apply silicone caulk between the floor and obstacle.

Tip: To reverse directions of the tongue and groove for doorways, glue a spline into the groove of the board. Fit the groove of the next board onto the spline, then nail the board in place.

How to Install a Decorative Medallion

1 Place the medallion on the floor where you want it installed. Draw a line around the medallion onto the floor.

2 Nail the installation jig to the floor so the opening is aligned with the outline you drew in the previous step. Drive the nails into joints in the floor.

3 Using the router bit that came with the medallion, place the bearing of the router bit on the inside edge of the jig opening and make a ¼"-deep cut. Remove any exposed nails or staples. Make repeated passes with the router, gradually increasing the depth, until you reach the subfloor.

4 Use a pry bar to remove the flooring inside the hole. Remove all nails. Dry-fit the medallion to ensure it fits. Remove the jig and fill nail holes with wood putty.

5 Apply urethane flooring adhesive to the subfloor where the hardwood was removed. Spread the adhesive with a trowel. Set the medallion in place and push it firmly into the adhesive so it's level with the surrounding floor.

1 To establish a straight layout line, snap a chalk line parallel to the longest wall, about 30" from the wall. Kneel in this space to begin flooring installation.

2 Apply flooring adhesive to the subfloor on the other side of the layout line with a notched trowel, according to the manufacturer's directions. Take care not to obscure the layout line with adhesive.

3 Apply wood glue to the grooved end of each piece as you install it to help joints stay tight. Do not apply glue to the long sides of boards.

4 Install the first row of flooring with the edge of the tongues directly over the chalk line. Make sure end joints are tight, then wipe up any excess glue immediately. At walls, leave a ½" space to allow for expansion of the wood. This gap will be covered by the baseboard and base shoe.

5 For succeeding rows, insert the tongue into the groove of the preceding row, and pivot the flooring down into the adhesive. Gently slide the tongue and groove ends together. At walls, use a hammer and a flooring pull bar to draw together the joints on the last strip (inset).

6 After you've installed three or four rows, use a mallet and scrap piece of flooring to gently tap boards together, closing up the seams. All joints should fit tightly.

7 Use a cardboard template to fit boards in irregular areas. Cut cardboard to match the space, and allow for a ½" expansion gap next to the wall. Trace the template outline on a board, then cut it to fit using a jig saw. Finish layering strips over the entire floor.

8 Bond the flooring to the adhesive by rolling it with a heavy floor roller. Roll the flooring within 3 hours of the adhesive application. Work in sections, and finish by installing the flooring in the section between your starting line and the wall.

Herringbone floors can lend a rustic look (above) or a formal, decorative feel to a room (right). Herringbone is available in different sizes to meet your design needs.

Installing Parquet Flooring

When you want to get away from a linear floor pattern but want to stick with hardwood, parquet floors are the perfect option. They offer more pizzazz than strip flooring without sacrificing the beauty and elegance of wood.

Parquet comes in a variety of patterns and styles to create geometric designs. It can range from elaborate, custom-designed patterns on the high end, to the more common herringbone pattern, to the widely available and less expensive block design.

Parquet has experienced a radical transformation over the years. A few years ago, each individual piece of parquet was hand-cut and painstak-

ingly assembled piece by piece. Today, parquet is prefabricated so the individual pieces making up the design are available as single tiles, which not only has reduced the cost, but has made the flooring easier to install.

One aspect that hasn't changed is the formal appeal of parquet. It's still relegated mostly to formal rooms, such as a dining area, although it has been used in foyers and entryways to create a stately appearance.

As with other wood floors, parquet is sensitive to moisture and changes in humidity. Parquet is also available in engineered wood, which can

The captivating designs provided by parquet floors are unrivaled by any other hardwood flooring (above, below, opposite page). Despite the complexities of individual patterns, modern parquet floors are installed the same way: panels set in adhesive.

withstand changes in temperature and humidity better than traditional wood flooring.

There are many types and designs of parquet floors, from custom-made originals to standard patterns, but they're all installed the same way—set in adhesive on a wood subfloor. Although the sequence for laying out parquet panels is similar to ceramic tile, the installation is a bit different. The panels are placed firmly in adhesive without the sliding and twisting associated with ceramic tile installation.

Remember to acclimate the parquet to the room before installation. When installing parquet, be sure the first few panels are aligned perfectly, since they set the pattern for the rest of the floor. Some of the more sophisticated patterns and larger blocks have square edges that butt together. Other parquet floor coverings, such as the "finger block" pattern shown on pages 104 to 106, feature a tongue-and-groove design for fastening the panels together.

Parquet can be used to create shapes and decorations not possible with other wood flooring.

The finger block pattern is one of the most widely available parquet coverings and also one of the least expensive. The configuration of perpendicular strips of wood emphasizes the different grains and natural color variations.

Herringbone, shown on page 107, is different than other parquets. It comes in tongue-and-groove strips that fit together at right angles. There are right and left side strips that are differentiated by their tongue-and-groove positions. Herringbone is not as popular as it once was, primarily due to the expense involved in installation. It takes longer to install than other flooring, resulting in higher costs from professional installers. By doing it yourself, you eliminate those costs and end up with a sensational floor.

Tools & Materials:

Tape measure, chalk line, carpenter's square, parquet flooring, adhesive, notched trowel, putty knife, rubber mallet, 100- to 150-pound floor roller, jig saw, solvent.

Photo courtesy of Oshkosh Floor Designs

Photo courtesy of Kentucky Wood Floors

How to Install Parquet Flooring

1 Mark the centerpoint of each wall. Snap chalk lines between the marks on opposite walls to establish your reference lines. Use the 3-4-5 triangle method to check the lines for squareness (see page 80).

2 Lay out a dry run of panels from the center point along the reference lines to adjacent walls. If more than half of the last panel needs to be cut off, adjust the lines by half the width of the panel. Snap new working lines, if necessary.

3 Put enough adhesive on the subfloor for your first panel, using a putty knife. Spread the adhesive into a thin layer with a notched trowel held at a 45° angle. Apply the adhesive right up to the working lines, but don't cover them.

4 Place the first panel on the adhesive so two sides are flush with the working lines. Don't slide or twist the panel when setting it into place. It's crucial for this panel to be positioned correctly to keep the rest of your floor square.

Variation: If the floor will continue down a hallway, do a dry run with the flooring before applying any adhesive. If the last panels have to be cut by more than half their width, adjust the starting lines accordingly.

5 Apply enough adhesive for six to eight panels and spread it with a notched trowel.

6 Set the next panel in place by holding it at a 45° angle and locking the tongue-and-groove joints with the first panel. Lower the panel onto the adhesive without sliding it. Install remaining panels the same way.

7 After every six to eight panels are installed, tap them into the adhesive with a rubber mallet.

(continued next page)

8 For the last row, align panels over the top of the last installed row. Place a third row over the top of these, with the sides butted against ½" spacers along the wall. Draw a line along the edge of the third panels onto the second row, cut the panels at the marks, and install.

9 When installing flooring around corners or obstacles, align a panel over the last installed panel, then place another panel on top of it as in step 8. Keep the top panel ½" from the wall or obstacle and trace along the opposite edge onto the second panel (top). Move the top two panels to the adjoining side, making sure not to turn the top panel. Make a second mark on the panel the same way (bottom). Cut the tile with a jig saw and install.

Tip: If you happen to get adhesive on your panels, clean it off immediately before it dries. Use a solvent recommended by the adhesive manufacturer.

10 Within 4 hours of installing the floor, roll the floor with a 100- to 150-pound floor roller. Wait at least 24 hours before walking on the floor again.

How to Install Parquet Using a Diagonal Layout

1 Establish perpendicular working lines following Step 1 on page 104. Measure 5 ft. from the centerpoint along each working line and make a mark. Snap chalk lines between the 5 ft. marks. Mark the centerpoint of these lines, then snap a chalk line through the marks to create a diagonal reference line.

2 Lay out a dry run of tiles along a diagonal line. Adjust your starting point as necessary. Lay the flooring along the diagonal line using adhesive, following the steps for installing parquet (pages 104 to 106). Make paper templates for tile along walls and in corners. Transfer the template measurements to tiles, and cut to fit.

How to Install Flooring Using a Herringbone Pattern

1 Snap perpendicular working lines and a diagonal line following step 1 above. Spread a small amount of adhesive on the sub-floor. NOTE: there are right-side and left-side panels differentiated by their tongue and groove locations. Place the top corner of a left-side panel along a working line. Use a framing square to make sure the side of the panel is square to the diagonal line.

2 Place the groove on the end of a right-side panel over the tongue on the side of the first panel so the outside edges are flush.

3 Place a right-side panel (A) along the right outside edge of the two installed panels. Align the top edge with the outside edge of the first left side panel. A left-side panel (B) is placed along these, then a right-side panel (C). Repeat this process, locking the tongue-and-groove joints together, for the remainder of the floor.

Installing End Grain Floors

It's hard to look at these floors and not be impressed. End grain, also known as cobble wood, is a specialty floor covering with a very distinctive look. The "bricks" resemble masonry bricks, but they're actually end grains cut from new and antique timbers. The result is a majestic floor with a rich, bold character.

End grain is mainly available in oak and pine, although other species of wood can be used. The project on the following pages uses ash and the block pattern uses apple. Each end grain brick is hand sanded, hand beveled, and sealed. The wood has natural cracks and splits, which is part of its appeal. The bricks are also grouted, like tile, making this wood product truly original.

Homeowners have mainly used end grain in

their kitchens and hallways, although it can installed in any room where you want the floor to create a sensation.

As high-end floor coverings, end grain is some of the most expensive floor products on the market. It can cost up to $40 per square foot with installation, although some patterns are less expensive. You can save a lot of money by installing it

yourself and end up with the same great look.

End grain installation is more time consuming than other wood floor coverings, but it's worth the extra effort. You'll end up with an extraordinary floor that's built to last.

Installing end grain is similar to installing tile. It's installed on cementboard, set in adhesive, and grouted. Each brick has a slightly different shape than the next, so spacers cannot be used to establish grout lines. Instead, space the bricks by eye, maintaining consistent grout lines, and aligning every sixth row with your working lines. The bricks are treated by the manufacturer so they won't absorb the grout or the grout sealer.

As with other floors, it's imperative to have a level subfloor. If the cementboard is uneven, the bricks may not lie flat and the grout will eventually crack. Even with a good subfloor, you may find it's necessary to regrout the bricks every several years. Make sure to use a grout with an acrylic additive that can fill large grout lines. Some grouts, for example, are only recommended for $\frac{1}{8}$" grout lines.

The project on the following pages shows how to install a cobblewood floor using a traditional running bond pattern. You can use other patterns, such as the two-brick basket weave and hexagonal, or herringbone, patterns shown on page 112.

Regardless of the pattern you use, the installation procedures are the same. Before applying adhesive, make sure to do a test run with the bricks to see exactly how the pattern will layout. You don't want any surprises once your adhesive is down.

The end grain blocks shown on page 113 is installed similar to end grain bricks, except you have more flexibility in your layout and you don't have to follow reference lines. It's still important to conduct a dry run prior to installation to get a good mix of timbers. Try to keep the distance between the blocks as consistent as possible.

Tools & Materials

Tape measure, chalk line, framing square, thinset, cobblewood, grout with acrylic additives, grout sealer, cementboard, 1¼" deck screws, cordless drill, slide compound saw, rubber grout float, grout sponge, dry cloth, sponge brush, ¼" notched trowel, thin-set with acrylic additives.

How to Install End Grain Brick Flooring

1 Cover the floor with cementboard set in thin-set mortar and fastened to the subfloor with 1¼" cementboard screws (see page 60).

2 Establish perpendicular working lines, following step 1 on page 104. Establish another reference line from your vertical working line that's half the length of the end grain brick and half the width of a grout line.

3 Place six bricks along the vertical lines in a dry run. Measure the distance from the top of the first brick to the bottom of the last brick, plus ¼" for each grout line, then snap a series of parallel lines at that measurement to help keep the bricks running straight.

4 Spread thin-set adhesive along the working lines in one of the middle quadrants for two rows of bricks.

5 Place the bricks firmly in the thin-set. The bricks should be flush with the working lines and separated by grout lines. Set the rest of floor the same way. Allow the floor to sit for 24 hours.

Tip: To cut end grain bricks, mark the brick, then cut along the line using a slide compound saw. Seal the cut edge with an oil based finish.

6 Mix the grout following the manufacturer's directions. Use a grout with acrylic additives.

7 Starting in a corner, apply the grout onto the bricks. Spread the grout outward from the corner using a rubber grout float. Hold the float at a 60° angle and press firmly to completely fill the joints.

(continued next page)

8 Wipe away excess grout, using a damp grout sponge. Wipe diagonally across the bricks, covering each joint only once to avoid removing grout between the bricks. Rinse the sponge in water often. Allow the grout to dry for 4 hours.

9 Use a soft, dry cloth to clean the bricks. Buff the surface until it's free of grout and doesn't have a waxy film.

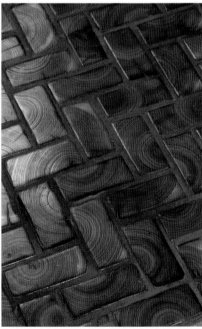

10 Use a small sponge brush to apply grout sealer to the grout lines. Apply just enough sealer to wet the grout. Wipe any sealer off the bricks immediately with a cloth.

Basket Weave Variation: Place the bricks in pairs with two bricks running vertically, then two bricks running horizontally. Align the outside edges of the bricks.

Herringbone Pattern Variation: Alternate between vertical and horizontal bricks. Place the first brick horizontally along a working line, place a vertical brick next to it, then place the next vertical brick at half that height. Repeat this pattern across the floor, keeping the outside edges flush.

How to Install End Grain Block Flooring

1 Cover the subfloor with cementboard, following step 1 on page 110. Starting at the center of the floor, lay out several blocks in a dry run. Gaps between blocks will vary in size, but try to keep them as small as possible.

2 Spread thin-set adhesive onto the floor and press the blocks firmly in place. Continue to dry fit the blocks in place to find good fits before applying thin-set.

3 Once the blocks have set for 24 hours, spread grout into the joints using a rubber grout float. Wipe away excess grout and seal the grout lines following steps 8-10 on the opposite page.

4 Apply grout sealer to the grout lines, using a sponge brush. Apply enough sealer to wet the grout. If sealer gets on the blocks, wipe it away immediately, using a cloth.

Installing Floating Floors

Floor installation doesn't get any easier than this. Floating floors have revolutionized the way floor coverings are installed, no longer requiring nails, staples, tackless strips, or adhesive. The advent of floating floors with their special tongue-and-groove fastening system has helped flooring become a popular do-it-yourself project rather than a job for professionals.

Floating floors are most often associated with laminates, although other products can be used. Cork, which is shown below and on pages 118 to 120, is a fashionable choice for floating floors and just as easy to install.

Part of the appeal of floating floors is that they don't require a special subfloor. The actual floor covering is not fastened or adhered to the sub-floor in any way. Instead, it "floats" above the subfloor and is held in place solely by its own weight.

This technology allows you to install a floating floor over most existing floors. Floating floors simply click together at the tongue and groove joints. The process allows for exceptionally quick installation, and you can walk on the floor immediately after you're done.

Another reason for floating floors' popularity is their sleek appearance. The laminates replicate the look of hardwoods, while cork offers a look all its own. Unlike the surfaces they emulate, floating floors are resistant to scratching, denting, fading, scuffing, staining, and burning, so they're easier to maintain.

Photo courtesy of Natural Cork

The grain pattern in the laminate floor on the left features the look of real wood and harmonizes with the wood accessories in the room. The above floor is composed of cork. Both floors "float" above the subfloor.

Keep in mind where the floating floor will be located. It's not a good idea to install it in a bathroom where it will be exposed to moisture or an entryway where people will place their wet shoes or boots. Although floating floors are impervious to scratches and scuff marks, they are not resistant to water. After the floor is installed, apply caulk along the bottom edge of panels that could come into contact with water, such as in front of a dishwasher, sink, or exterior door.

Installing floating floors is simple and quick, and doesn't require any messy adhesives. While a sturdy, level subfloor is needed, you don't need to invest a lot of time preparing the subfloor or installing cementboard or isolation membrane.

Floating floors are installed over underlayment that's rolled out the length of the floor. With some floating floors, the underlayment is not needed at all, which eliminates yet another step in the installation process. Instead, the flooring panels have a pad already installed on the bottom side that serves as the underlayment. Not only does the underlayment provide a cushion under the

floor, it serves as a sound barrier and helps reduce noises between rooms.

Some panels, such as the cork flooring shown on the following pages, lock together without using glue in the connections. Other panels have glue already applied to the tongues. Once the joints are snapped together, the friction heats up the glue and helps secure the connection. Page 121 shows how to apply glue to panels that require glue in the joints.

The joints on floating floors fit together very tightly. They don't have gaps between panels the way hardwood flooring does, so you never have to worry about dirty seams or debris getting stuck in your floor.

Tools & Materials:

Tape measure, underlayment, utility knife, floor panels, circular saw, straightedge, hammer, floor tool bar, chalk, chalk gun, jig saw, glue.

One of the nice features of laminated floating floor planks (above and below left) is that decorative imprints can be ingrained in the flooring. The floating floor below mimics the look of real wood.

Photos this page courtesy of Pergo, Inc., www.pergo.com

How to Install a Floating Floor

1 Choose the manufacturer's recommended underlayment and roll it out to fit the entire floor. Do not overlap seams.

2 Place ½" spacers along the starting wall to provide a gap for expansion of the flooring. Set the first row of flooring against the spacers with the groove side facing the wall.

3 Install successive rows of flooring by lifting the panels at a 45° angle and sliding them into the tongue of the preceding panels until they lock into place. Stagger joints by at least 8".

4 After locking the long edge of the panel in place, slide the panel back to fit the short edge into the tongue of the last panel in the row. Use a mallet and scrap piece of wood to gently tap it into place.

5 At the end of the rows, use a floor pull bar and hammer to fit the last board into place. Leave a ½" gap along walls.

Cut panels by turning the panel face down. Mark the appropriate length, then cut along the mark using a circular saw. Cut-off pieces can be used to begin the next row, provided they are at least 10" long.

(continued next page)

6 For the last row of flooring, place panels directly over the last installed row. Place a third panel on top of the second and butt the side against the ½" spacers along the wall. Trace along the edge of the panel onto the second panel, then cut the second panel to size.

7 Set the last row of panels in place. If needed, use the floor pull bar to pull the panels in place.

8 Apply a bead of caulk along the edge of the flooring to prevent water intrusion.

To fit panels around obstacles place the board next to the obstacle, mark it, and cut it with a jig saw. Set the board in place by locking the tongue-and-groove joints with the preceding board.

How to Install a Floating Floor Using Glue

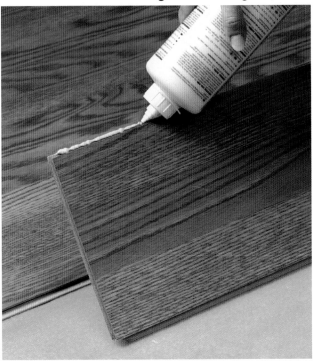

1 Follow the same installation process for glueless floors, but rather than locking the tongue-and-groove connections, apply the manufacturer's recommended glue to the grooves in the planks. Be sure to also glue the end joints.

2 Place the groove in the plank over the tongue of the preceding plank. Place a scrap piece of wood against the plank and use a mallet to tap it into place. Install remaining planks the same way.

3 Wipe away excess glue in the joints with a damp cloth before it dries.

Moisten the tongues on pre-glued planks with water, then slide them into the grooves of the preceeding planks.

Ceramic, Stone & Resilient Flooring

Ceramic, stone, and resilient tiles allow you to incorporate elaborate designs and patterns into your floor. They also enable you to use different colors to create a striking visual effect. You can use the grout lines of ceramic and stone tiles to complement or contrast tile colors for added appeal.

These floor coverings and resilient sheet flooring are primarily used in kitchens, baths, and hallways. Since they're resistant to water and moisture, they are ideal for rooms in which hardwood and carpeting cannot be used. Marble tile and other high-end tiles are also used in formal settings, such as living and dining rooms.

This section includes directions for the installation of ceramic tile and resilient flooring. Resilient tile with self-adhesive is probably the quickest and easiest type of covering to install. Once the reference lines are established, the paper backing is removed and the tiles are placed on the floor. Resilient sheet flooring requires an adhesive to be spread on the floor, but installation is still relatively fast. Ceramic tiles are placed in thin-set mortar and grouted.

Installation for ceramic and resilient tiles starts with the same process of establishing reference lines through the center of the room and test-fitting tiles to create the perfect layout. As with other floor coverings, ceramic and resilient flooring require a carefully prepared underlayment to ensure a professional-looking finish.

When choosing ceramic tiles or resilient coverings, look for a surface that's slip-resistant. Ceramic tile that is textured or soft-glazed can protect against slips as well as staining.

Resilient floors offer traditional or contemporary designs to fit your room's style. The floor at the top contains a decorative pattern imitating the look of ceramic tile and grout. The bright blue in the bedroom floor (bottom) provides the right amount of contrast to the white walls.

Resilient Flooring

Resilient flooring has come a long way since the old linoleum floors. Today's vinyl floors can mimic ceramic, stone, and terrazzo with remarkable realism.

Resilient flooring products are made from a variety of materials. Vinyl is the most popular resilient covering, although rubber and cork materials are also used. Vinyl flooring is available in both sheets and tiles in thicknesses ranging from ⅟₁₆" to ⅛". The sheets come in 6-foot-wide and 12-foot-wide rolls and have either a felt or a PVC backing, depending on the type of installation. Tiles typically come in 12" or 16" squares and are available with or without self-adhesive backing.

Installation of resilient flooring is easier than most other floor coverings. Sheet vinyl with felt backing is glued to the floor using the full-spread method, meaning the entire project area is covered with adhesive, then the floor is placed on the adhesive. PVC-backed sheet vinyl is glued only along the edges, which is called perimeter-bond. Vinyl tiles are the easiest to install, but because these tile floors have many seams, they're less suitable for high-moisture areas.

Sheet vinyl is priced per square yard, while vinyl tile is priced per square foot. The cost for either is comparable to carpet and less expensive than ceramic tile or hardwood. Prices vary based on the percentage of vinyl in the material, the thickness of the product, and the complexity of the pattern.

Whether you're installing vinyl in sheets or tiles, it must be placed over a smooth underlayment. Any debris or defects in the underlayment will show through the floor covering.

Photo courtesy of Marmoleum by Forbo Linoleum

This kitchen floor combines several colors for a stimulating design.

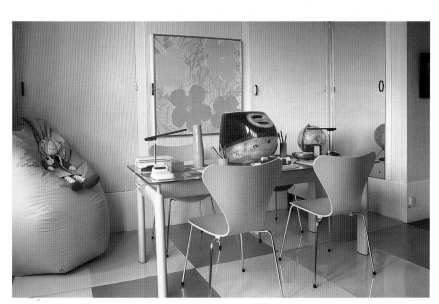

The vivid colors in this resilient floor match the furniture and overall decor of the room.

Preparation Tools & Materials

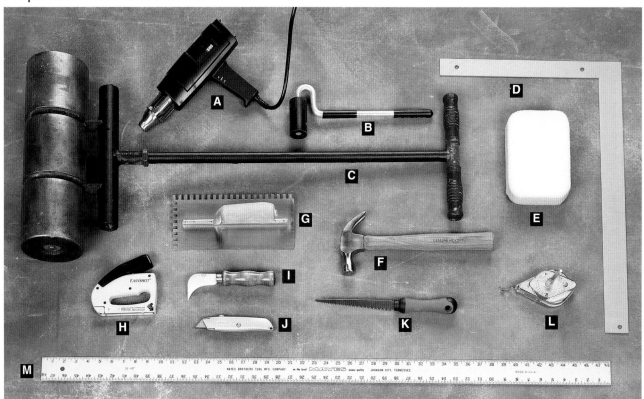

Tools for resilient flooring include: a heat gun (A), J-roller (B), floor roller (C), framing square (D), sponge (E), hammer (F), notched trowel (G), stapler (H), linoleum knife (I), utility knife (J), wallboard knife (K), chalk line (L), straightedge (M).

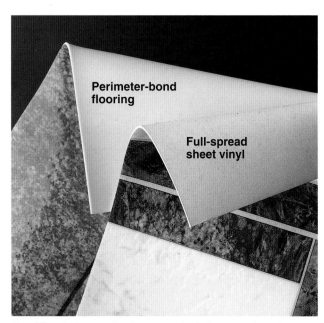

Resilient sheet vinyl comes in full-spread and perimeter-bond styles. Full-spread sheet vinyl has a felt-paper backing and is secured with adhesive that's spread over the floor before installation. Perimeter-bond flooring, identifiable by its smooth, white PVC backing, is laid directly on underlayment and is secured by a special adhesive spread along the edges and seams.

Resilient tile comes in self-adhesive and dry-back styles. Self-adhesive tile has a pre-applied adhesive protected by wax paper backing that's peeled off as the tiles are installed. Dry-back tile is secured with adhesive spread onto the underlayment before installation. Self-adhesive tile is easier to install than dry-back tile, but the bond is less reliable. Don't use additional adhesives with self-adhesive tile.

Tip for Resilient Flooring

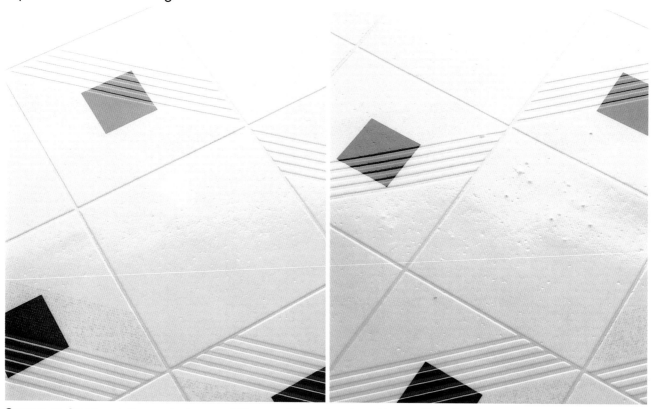

Sweep and vacuum the underlayment thoroughly before installing resilient flooring to ensure a smooth, flawless finish (left). Small pieces of debris can create noticeable bumps in the flooring (right).

Handle resilient sheet vinyl carefully to avoid creasing or tearing (inset). Working with a helper can help prevent costly mistakes. Make sure the sheet vinyl is at room temperature before you handle it.

Most resilient flooring is made, at least in part, from vinyl. In general, the higher the percentage of vinyl in the product, the higher the quality of the floor. In solid vinyl flooring, the design pattern is built up from solid layers of vinyl. Vinyl composition flooring combines vinyl with filler materials. Printed vinyl flooring relies on a screen print for its color and pattern. The print is protected by a vinyl-and-urethane wear layer.

Installing Resilient Sheet Vinyl

Preparing a perfect underlayment is the most important phase of resilient sheet vinyl installation. Cutting the material to fit the contours of the room is a close second. The best way to ensure accurate cuts is to make a cutting template. Some manufacturers offer template kits, or you can make one by following the instructions on the opposite page. Be sure to use the recommended adhesive for the sheet vinyl you are installing. Many manufacturers require that you use their glue for installation. Use extreme care when handling the sheet vinyl, especially felt-backed products, to avoid creasing and tearing.

Tools & Materials:

Linoleum knife, framing square, compass, scissors, non-permanent felt-tipped pen, utility knife, straightedge, ¼" V-notched trowel, J-roller, stapler, flooring roller, chalk line, heat gun, ⅟₁₆" V-notched trowel, straightedge, vinyl flooring, masking tape, heavy butcher or brown wrapping paper, duct tape, flooring adhesive, ⅜" staples, metal threshold bars, nails.

How to Cut Vinyl

Use a linoleum knife or utility knife and a straightedge to cut resilient flooring. Make sure to use a sharp knife blade, and change blades often. Always make cuts on a smooth surface, such as a scrap of hardboard placed under the flooring.

How to Make a Cutting Template

1 Place sheets of heavy butcher paper or brown wrapping paper along the walls, leaving a ⅛" gap. Cut triangular holes in the paper with a utility knife. Fasten the template to the floor by placing masking tape over the holes.

2 Follow the outline of the room, working with one sheet of paper at a time. Overlap the edges of adjoining sheets by about 2" and tape the sheets together.

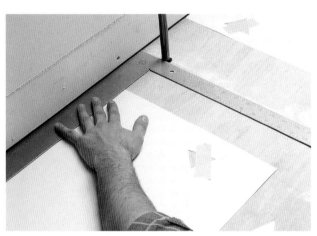

3 To fit the template around pipes, tape sheets of paper on either side. Measure the distance from the wall to the center of the pipe, then subtract ⅛".

4 Transfer the measurement to a separate piece of paper. Use a compass to draw the pipe diameter on the paper, then cut out the hole with scissors or a utility knife. Cut a slit from the edge of the paper to the hole.

5 Fit the hole cutout around the pipe. Tape the hole template to the adjoining sheets.

6 When completed, roll or loosely fold the paper template for carrying.

How to Install Perimeter-bond Sheet Vinyl

1 Unroll the flooring on any large, flat, clean surface. To prevent wrinkles, sheet vinyl comes from the manufacturer rolled with the pattern side out. Unroll the sheet and turn it pattern-side up for marking.

2 For two-piece installations, overlap the edges of the sheets by at least 2". Plan to have the seams fall along the pattern lines or simulated grout joints. Align the sheets so the pattern matches, then tape the sheets together with duct tape.

3 Position the paper template over the sheet vinyl and tape it in place. Trace the outline of the template onto the flooring using a non-permanent felt-tipped pen.

4 Remove the template. Cut the sheet vinyl with a sharp linoleum knife or a utility knife with a new blade. Use a straightedge as a guide for making longer cuts.

5 Cut holes for pipes and other permanent obstructions. Cut a slit from each hole to the nearest edge of the flooring. Whenever possible, make slits along pattern lines.

6 Roll up the flooring loosely and transfer it to the installation area. Do not fold the flooring. Unroll and position the sheet vinyl carefully. Slide the edges beneath undercut door casings.

7 Cut the seams for two-piece installations using a straightedge as a guide. Hold the straightedge tightly against the flooring, and cut along the pattern lines through both pieces of vinyl flooring.

8 Remove both pieces of scrap flooring. The pattern should now run continuously across the adjoining sheets of flooring.

(continued next page)

9 Fold back the edges of both sheets. Apply a 3" band of multipurpose flooring adhesive to the underlayment or old flooring, using a ¼" V-notched trowel or wallboard knife.

10 Lay the seam edges one at a time onto the adhesive. Make sure the seam is tight, pressing the gaps together with your fingers, if needed. Roll the seam edges with a J-roller or wallpaper seam roller.

11 Apply flooring adhesive underneath flooring cuts at pipes or posts and around the entire perimeter of the room. Roll the flooring with the roller to ensure good contact with the adhesive.

12 If you're applying flooring over a wood underlayment, fasten the outer edges of the sheet with ⅜" staples driven every 3". Make sure the staples will be covered by the base molding.

How to Install Full-spread Sheet Vinyl

1 Cut the sheet vinyl using the techniques described on pages 130 and 131 (steps 1 to 5), then lay the sheet vinyl into position, sliding the edges under door casings.

2 Pull back half of the flooring, then apply a layer of flooring adhesive over the underlayment or old flooring using a ¼" V-notched trowel. Lay the flooring back onto the adhesive.

3 Roll the floor with a heavy flooring roller, moving toward the edges of the sheet. The roller creates a stronger bond and eliminates air bubbles. Fold over the unbonded section of flooring, apply adhesive, then replace and roll the flooring. Wipe up any adhesive that oozes up around the edges of the vinyl, using a damp rag.

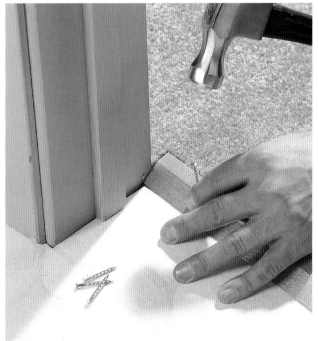

4 Measure and cut metal threshold bars to fit across doorways. Position each bar over the edge of the vinyl flooring and nail it in place.

Installing Resilient Tile

As with any tile installation, resilient tile requires carefully positioned layout lines. Before committing to any layout and applying tile, conduct a dry run to identify potential problems.

Keep in mind there's a difference between reference lines (see opposite page) and layout lines (see page 136). Reference lines mark the center of the room and divide it into quadrants. If the tiles don't layout out symmetrically along these lines, you'll need to adjust them slightly, creating layout lines.

Once layout lines are established, installing the tile is fairly quick, especially if you're using self-adhesive tile. Be sure to keep joints between the tiles tight and lay the tiles square.

Tiles with an obvious grain pattern can be laid so the grain of each tile is oriented identically throughout the installation. You can also use the quarter-turn method, in which each tile has its pattern grain running perpendicular to that of adjacent tiles. Whichever method you choose, be sure to be consistent throughout the project.

Tools & Materials:

Tape measure, chalk line, framing square, utility knife, ⅟₁₆" notched trowel, heat gun, resilient tile, flooring adhesive (for dry-back tile).

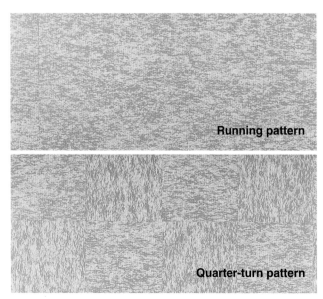

Check for noticeable directional features, like the grain of the vinyl particles. You can set the tiles in a running pattern so the directional feature runs in the same direction (top), or in a checkerboard pattern using the quarter-turn method (bottom).

Make curved cuts in thick, rigid resilient tile by heating the back of the tile with a heat gun, then cutting the tile while it's still warm.

How to Make Reference Lines for Tile Installation

1 Position a reference line (X) by measuring along opposite sides of the room and marking the center of each side. Snap a chalk line between these marks.

2 Measure and mark the centerpoint of the chalk line. From this point, use a framing square to establish a second reference line perpendicular to the first one. Snap the second line (Y) across the room.

3 Check the reference lines for squareness using the 3-4-5 triangle method. Measure along reference line X and make a mark 3 ft. from the centerpoint. Measure from the centerpoint along reference line Y and make a mark at 4 ft.

4 Measure the distance between the marks. If the reference lines are perpendicular, the distance will measure exactly 5 ft. If not, adjust the reference lines until they're exactly perpendicular to each other.

How to Establish Tile Layout Lines

1 Snap perpendicular reference lines with a chalk line. Dry-fit tiles along layout line Y so a joint falls along reference line X. If necessary, shift the layout to make the layout symmetrical or to reduce the number of tiles that need to be cut.

2 If you shift the tile layout, create a new line that's parallel to reference line X and runs through a tile joint near line X. The new line, X', is the line you'll use when installing the tile. To avoid confusion, use a different colored chalk to distinguish between lines.

3 Dry-fit tiles along the new line, X'. If necessary, adjust the layout line as in steps 1 and 2.

4 If you adjusted the layout along X', measure and make a new layout line, Y', that's parallel to reference line Y and runs through a tile joint. Y' will form the second layout line you'll use during installation.

How to Install Self-adhesive Resilient Tiles

1 Once your reference lines are established, peel off the paper backing and install the first tile in one of the corners formed by the intersecting layout lines. Lay three or more tiles along each layout line in the quadrant. Rub the entire surface of each tile to bond the adhesive to the floor underlayment.

2 Begin installing tiles in the interior area of the quadrant, keeping the joints tight between tiles.

3 Finish setting full tiles in the first quadrant, then set the full tiles in an adjacent quadrant. Set the tiles along the layout lines first, then fill in the interior tiles.

Note: Tile to be cut shown inverted for clarity; tiles should be faceup for marking.

4 To cut tiles to fit along the walls, place the tile to be cut (A) faceup on top of the last full tile you installed. Position a ⅛"-thick spacer against the wall, then set a marker tile (B) on top of the tile to be cut. Trace along the edge of the marker tile to draw a cutting line.

(continued next page)

Tip: To mark tiles for cutting around outside corners, make a cardboard template to match the space, keeping a ⅛" gap along the walls. After cutting the template, check to make sure it fits. Place the template on a tile and trace its outline.

5 Cut tile to fit using a utility knife and straightedge. Hold the straightedge securely against the cutting line to ensure a straight cut.

Option: You can use a ceramic-tile cutter to make straight cuts in thick vinyl tiles.

6 Install cut tiles next to the walls. If you're precutting all tiles before installing them, measure the distance between the wall and installed tiles at various points in case the distance changes.

7 Continue installing tile in the remaining quadrants until the room is completely covered. Check the entire floor. If you find loose areas, press down on the tiles to bond them to the underlayment. Install metal threshold bars at room borders where the new floor joins another floor covering.

How to Install Dry-back Tile

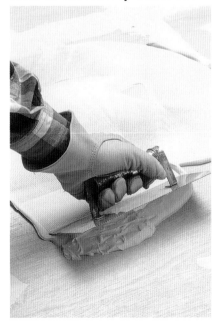

1 Create perpendicular reference lines and dry-lay tiles to establish the final layout. Apply adhesive around the intersection of the layout lines using a trowel with ¹⁄₁₆" V-shaped notches. Hold the trowel at a 45° angle and spread adhesive evenly over the surface.

2 Spread adhesive over most of the installation area, covering three quadrants. Allow the adhesive to set according to the manufacturer's instructions, then begin to install the tile at the intersection of the layout lines. You can kneel on installed tiles to lay additional tiles. When the first three quadrants are completely tiled, spread adhesive over the remaining quadrant, then finish setting the tile.

Ceramic & Stone Tile

Ceramic tile includes a wide variety of hard flooring products made from molded clay. Although there are significant differences between various types, they are all installed using cement-based mortar as an adhesive and grout to fill the gaps between tiles. These same techniques are used to install tiles cut from natural stone, such as granite and marble.

Ceramic and stone are the hardest of all floor coverings. With few exceptions, they are also the most expensive. Their durability, however, makes them worth the extra cost.

To ensure a long-lasting tile floor, you'll need a smooth, stable, and level subfloor (see page 37). In addition, the underlayment must be solid. Cementboard, or the thinner fiber/cementboard, is the best underlayment since it has excellent stability and is unaffected by moisture. Cementboard is manufactured exclusively for ceramic tile installation (see page 60). In rooms where moisture is not a factor, exterior-grade plywood is an adequate underlayment. It's also less expensive.

Another option is isolation membrane, which is used to protect ceramic tile and stone from movements caused by cracks in concrete floors. Isolation membrane is used to cover individual cracks, or it can be used to cover an entire floor. Page 61 shows how to install isolation membrane.

Many ceramic tiles have a glazed surface that protects the porous clay from staining. You should protect unglazed ceramic tile from stains and water spots by periodically applying a coat of tile sealer. Keep dirt from getting trapped in grout lines by sealing them once a year.

The most common adhesive for ceramic tile is thin-set mortar, which comes as a dry powder that's mixed with water. Pre-mixed organic adhesives generally are not recommended for floors.

Tile flooring should be durable and slip-resistant. Look for floor tile that is textured or soft-glazed for slip resistance and has a class or group

Photo courtesy of Buddy Rhodes Studio

A decorative border surrounds the island in the above kitchen while the field tiles match the countertops. The floor tile in the bathroom below carries on a color and design theme that repeats throughout the room.

rating of 3, 4, or 5 for strength. Floor tile should also be glazed for protection against staining.

If you use unglazed tile, be sure to seal it properly after installation. Standard grouts need stain-protection too. Mix your grout with a latex additive, and apply a grout sealer after the new grout sets. Reapply the sealer once a year thereafter.

A quality tile installation can last decades, so be sure to choose colors and designs with long-lasting appeal. Trendy styles can look dated in a few years. Tiles are available in a diverse range of shapes and sizes. Square tiles can make a room look larger, and they have fewer grout lines, making them easy to maintain. Irregular tile shapes, including rectangles, hexagons, and octagons, have spaces between tiles that are often filled with smaller diamond or square-shaped tiles.

For a more decorative floor, accent tiles such as mosaic borders and printed glazed tiles can be used as continuous borders or placed individually among the other tiles. Mosaic tiles come in unglazed porcelain and glazed ceramic varieties. They are installed in sheets held together with paper gauze backing or plastic webbing.

If you want to install trim tiles, consider their placement as you plan the layout. Some base-trim tile is set on the floor, with its finished edge flush with the field tile. Other types are installed on top of the field tile, after the field tile is laid and grouted.

Tools & Materials:

Chalk line, ¼" square-notched trowel, rubber mallet, tile-cutting tools (see pages 146 to 147), needlenose pliers, utility knife, grout float, grout sponge, buff rag, foam brush, tile, thin-set mortar, tile spacers, 2 × 4, threshold material, grout, latex additive (mortar and grout), grout sealer, silicone caulk.

Photo courtesy of Ceramic Tile of Italy

Field tile placed at a 45° angle, along with a decorative border and medallion, give the above floor instant appeal. Placing all of the tile at a 45° angle provides a basic design for the floor below and accentuates the room's simplistic style.

Photo courtesy of Ceramic Tile of Italy

Thin-set mortar is a fine-grained cement product used to bond floor tile to underlayment. It is prepared by adding liquid, a little at a time, to the dry powder and stirring the mixture to achieve a creamy consistency. Some mortars include a latex additive in the dry mix. With others, you'll need to add liquid latex additive when you prepare the mortar.

Ceramic Tile Tools & Materials

The tools required to cut tiles and to apply mortar and grout are generally small and fairly inexpensive.

The materials needed for tile installation include adhesive thin-set mortar, used to fasten the tiles to the underlayment; grout, used to fill the joints between tiles; and sealers, used to protect the tile surface and grout lines. Make sure to use the materials recommended by the tile manufacturer.

Trim and finishing materials for tile installation include base-trim tiles (A), which fit around the room perimeter, and bullnose tiles (B), used at doorways and other transition areas. Doorway thresholds (C) are made from synthetic materials as well as natural materials, such as marble, and come in thicknesses ranging from ¼" to ¾" to match different floor levels. The longest-lasting thresholds are made from solid-surface mineral products. If the threshold is too long for the doorway, cut it to fit with a jig saw or circular saw and a tungsten-carbide blade.

144

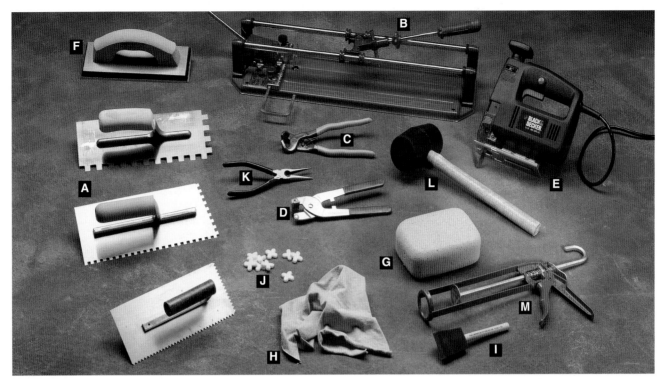

Tile tools include adhesive-spreading tools, cutting tools, and grouting tools. Notched trowels (A) for spreading mortar come with notches of varying sizes and shapes. The size of the notch should be proportional to the size of the tile being installed. Cutting tools include a tile cutter (B), tile nippers (C), hand-held tile cutter (D), and jig saw with carbide blade (E). Grouting tools include a grout float (F), grout sponge (G), buff rag (H), and foam brush (I), for applying grout sealer. Other tile tools include spacers (J), available in different sizes to create grout joints of varying widths; needlenose pliers (K), for removing spacers; rubber mallet (L), for setting tiles into mortar; and caulk gun (M).

Tile materials include adhesives, grouts, and sealers. Thin-set mortar (A), the most common floor-tile adhesive, is often strengthened with latex mortar additive (B). Grout additive (C) can be added to floor grout (D) to make it more resilient and durable. Grout fills the spaces between tiles and is available in pre-tinted colors to match your tile. Silicone caulk (E) should be used in place of grout where tile meets another surface, like a bathtub. Use wall-tile adhesive (F) for installing base-trim tile. Grout sealer (G) and porous-tile sealer (H) ward off stains and make maintenance easier.

How to Cut Tile Using a Tile Cutter

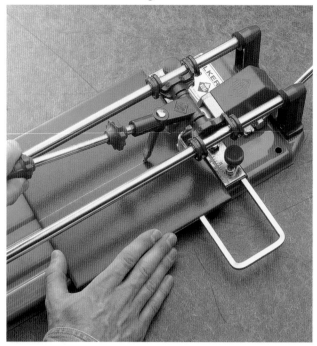

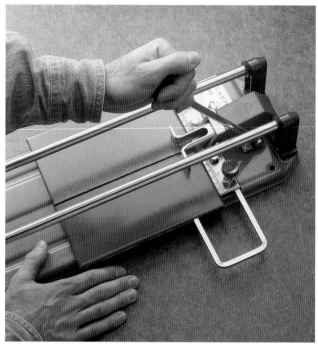

1 Mark a cutting line on the tile with a pencil, then place the tile in the cutter so the cutting wheel is directly over the line. While pressing down firmly on the wheel handle, run the wheel across the tile to score the surface. For a clean cut, score the tile only once.

2 Snap the tile along the scored line as directed by the tool manufacturer. Snapping the tile is usually accomplished by depressing a lever on the tile cutter.

How to Cut Tile Using Power Tools

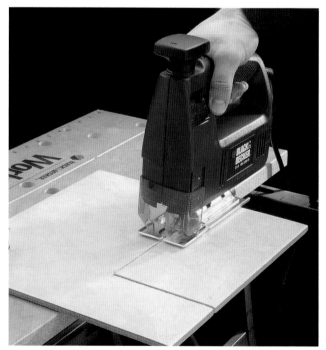

Tile saws, also called "wet saws" because they use water to cool blades and tiles, are used primarily for cutting natural-stone tiles. They're also useful for quickly cutting notches in all kinds of hard tile. Wet saws are available for rent at tile dealers and rental shops.

To make square notches, clamp the tile down on a worktable, then use a jig saw with a tungsten-carbide blade to make the cuts. If you need to cut several notches, a wet saw is more efficient.

How to Cut Tile Using Tile Nippers

1 Mark a cutting line on the tile face, then use the scoring wheel of a hand-held tile cutter to score the cut line. Make several parallel scores, no more than ¼" apart, in the waste portion of the tile.

2 Use tile nippers to nibble away the scored portion of the tile. To cut circular holes in the middle of a tile, score and cut the tile so it divides the hole in half, then remove waste material from each half of the circle.

Tips for Cutting Tile

To cut mosaic tiles, use a tile cutter to score tiles in the row where the cut will occur. Cut away excess strips of mosaics from the sheet, using a utility knife, then use a hand-held tile cutter to snap tiles one at a time. Use tile nippers to cut narrow portions of tiles after scoring.

Cut holes for plumbing stub-outs and other obstructions by marking the outline on the tile, then drilling around the edges using a ceramic tile bit (inset). Gently knock out the waste material with a hammer. The rough edges of the hole will be covered by protective plates on fixtures called "escutcheons."

Installing Ceramic Tile

Ceramic tile installation starts with the same steps as installing resilient tile. You snap perpendicular reference lines and dry-fit tiles to ensure the best placement.

When setting tiles, work in small sections so the mortar doesn't dry before the tiles are set. Use spacers between tiles to ensure consistent spacing. Plan an installation sequence to avoid kneeling on set tiles. Be careful not to kneel or walk on tiles until the designated drying period is over.

Tools & Materials:

¼" square trowel, rubber mallet, tile cutter, tile nippers, hand-held tile cutter, needlenose pliers, grout float, grout sponge, soft cloth, small paint brush, thin-set mortar, tile, tile spacers, grout, latex grout additive, wall adhesive, 2 × 4 lumber, grout sealer, tile caulk.

How to Install Ceramic Floor Tile

1 Make sure the subfloor is smooth, level, and stable. Spread thin-set mortar on the subfloor for one sheet of cementboard. Place the cementboard on the mortar, keeping a ¼" gap along the walls. Fasten it in place with 1¼" cementboard screws. Place fiberglass-mesh wallboard tape over the seams. Cover the remainder of the floor, following the steps on page 60.

2 Draw reference lines and establish the tile layout (see pages 135 to 136). Mix a batch of thin-set mortar, then spread the mortar evenly against both reference lines of one quadrant, using a ¼" square-notched trowel. Use the notched edge of the trowel to create furrows in the mortar bed.

3 Set the first tile in the corner of the quadrant where the reference lines intersect. When setting tiles that are 8" square or larger, twist each tile slightly as you set it into position.

4 Using a soft rubber mallet, gently tap the central area of each tile a few times to set it evenly into the mortar.

Variation: For large tiles or uneven stone, use a larger trowel with notches that are at least ½" deep.

Variation: For mosaic sheets, use a ³⁄₁₆" V-notched trowel to spread the mortar and a grout float to press the sheets into the mortar. Apply pressure gently to avoid creating an uneven surface.

(continued next page)

5 To ensure consistent spacing between tiles, place plastic tile spacers at the corners of the set tile. With mosaic sheets, use spacers equal to the gaps between tiles.

6 Position and set adjacent tiles into the mortar along the reference lines. Make sure the tiles fit neatly against the spacers.

7 To make sure the tiles are level with one another, place a straight piece of 2 × 4 across several tiles, then tap the board with a mallet.

8 Lay tile in the remaining area covered with mortar. Repeat steps 2 to 7, continuing to work in small sections, until you reach walls or fixtures.

9 Measure and mark tiles to fit against walls and into corners (see pages 137 to 138). Cut the tiles to fit. Apply thin-set mortar directly to the back of the cut tiles, instead of the floor, using the notched edge of the trowel to furrow the mortar.

10 Set the cut pieces of tile into position. Press down on the tile until each piece is level with adjacent tiles.

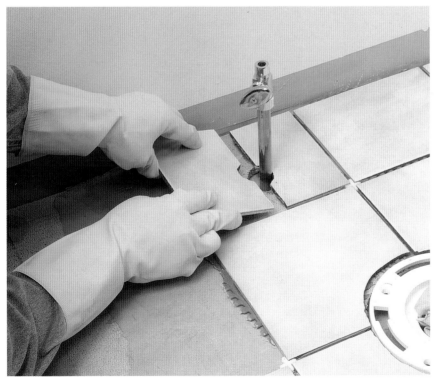

11 Measure, cut, and install tiles that require notches or curves to fit around obstacles, such as exposed pipes or toilet drains.

12 Carefully remove the spacers with needlenose pliers before the mortar hardens.

(continued next page)

13 Apply mortar and set tiles in the remaining quadrants, completing one quadrant before starting the next. Inspect all of the tile joints and use a utility knife or grout knife to remove any high spots of mortar that could show through the grout.

14 Install threshold material in doorways. If the threshold is too long for the doorway, cut it to fit with a jig saw or circular saw and a tungsten-carbide blade. Set the threshold in thin-set mortar so the top is even with the tile. Keep the same space between the threshold as between tiles. Let the mortar set for at least 24 hours.

15 Prepare a small batch of floor grout to fill the tile joints. When mixing grout for porous tile, such as quarry or natural stone, use an additive with a release agent to prevent grout from bonding to the tile surfaces.

16 Starting in a corner, pour the grout over the tile. Use a rubber grout float to spread the grout outward from the corner, pressing firmly on the float to completely fill the joints. For best results, tilt the float at a 60° angle to the floor and use a figure-eight motion.

17 Use the grout float to remove excess grout from the surface of the tile. Wipe diagonally across the joints, holding the float in a near-vertical position. Continue applying grout and wiping off excess until about 25 square feet of the floor has been grouted.

18 Wipe a damp grout sponge diagonally over about 2 square feet of the floor at a time. Rinse the sponge in cool water between wipes. Wipe each area only once since repeated wiping can pull grout back out of joints. Repeat steps 15 to 18 to apply grout to the rest of the floor.

19 Allow the grout to dry for about 4 hours, then use a soft cloth to buff the tile surface and remove any remaining grout film.

(continued next page)

How to Install Ceramic Floor Tile (continued)

20 Apply grout sealer to the grout lines, using a small sponge brush or sash brush. Avoid brushing sealer on to the tile surfaces. Wipe up any excess sealer immediately.

Variation: Use a tile sealer to seal porous tile, such as quarry tile or unglazed tile. Following the manufacturer's instructions, roll a thin coat of sealer over the tile and grout joints, using a paint roller and extension handle.

How to Install Base-trim Tile

1 Dry-fit the tiles to determine the best spacing. Grout lines in base tile do not always align with grout lines in the floor tile. Use rounded bullnose tiles at outside corners, and mark tiles for cutting as needed.

2 Leaving a ⅛" expansion gap between tiles at corners, mark any contour cuts necessary to allow the coved edges to fit together. Use a jig saw with a tungsten-carbide blade to make curved cuts.

3 Begin installing base-trim tiles at an inside corner. Use a notched trowel to apply wall adhesive to the back of the tile. Place ⅛" spacers on the floor under each tile to create an expansion joint.

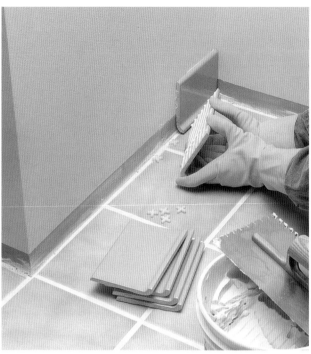

4 Press the tile onto the wall. Continue setting tiles, using spacers to maintain ⅛" gaps between the tiles and ⅛" expansion joints between the tiles and floor.

Double-bullnose tile

5 Use a double-bullnose tile on one side of outside corners to cover the edge of the adjoining tile.

6 After the adhesive dries, grout the vertical joints between tiles and apply grout along the tops of the tiles to make a continuous grout line. Once the grout hardens, fill the expansion joint between the tiles and floor with caulk.

A diagonal floor pattern is easy to install once you establish reference lines at a 45° angle to the original layout lines. Installation is similar to that of ordinary square tile, except the trim cuts will be diagonal.

Advanced Tile Techniques

Confident do-it-yourselfers who are familiar with basic tile techniques may be ready to undertake a project that's more challenging than a standard square tile floor installation. While the installations shown on the following pages usually require more time, the finished effect is well worth the extra effort.

Simply rotating the layout by 45° can yield striking results, as shown in the photo above. Offsetting the joints in adjacent tile rows to create a "running bond" pattern, a technique borrowed

from masonry and shown on page 159, also adds visual interest. A third method, shown on page 160, features a unique geometrical look using hexagonal tile. The final project, on page 161, is installing a tile border and employs a combination of techniques to create the look of an elegant area rug made of tile.

The advanced tile projects shown in this section assume a basic knowledge of tile installation. For this reason, the focus is on layout issues specific to certain tile shapes and desired effects.

Installing Borders on Floors

Borders add instant appeal to any floor. They can divide a floor into sections, or they can define a particular area of flooring, such as a mosaic. You can create a design inside the border by merely turning the tile at a 45° angle or installing decorative tiles. Designs with borders should cover between a quarter and half of the floor. If the design is too small, it'll get lost in the floor. If it's too big, it'll be distracting.

You'll need to determine the size and location of your border on paper, then transfer your measurements onto the floor. A dry run with the border and field tile is still required to ensure a smooth layout.

The tile is installed in three stages. The border is placed first, followed by outside field tile, then field tile within the border.

Photo courtesy of Crossville Porcelain Stone/USA

A border catches the eye and brings a creative element to the floor. Adding a border and using different colors for the tiles within the border bring the above floor to life.

How to Lay Out Borders

1 Measure the length and width of the room in which you'll be installing the border.

2 Transfer the measurements onto paper by making a scale drawing of the room. Include the locations of cabinets, doors, and furniture that will be in the room.

(continued next page)

How to Lay Out Borders (continued)

3 Determine the size of the border you want. Bordered designs should be between ¼ and ½ the area of the room. Draw the border on transparency paper, using the same scale as the room drawing.

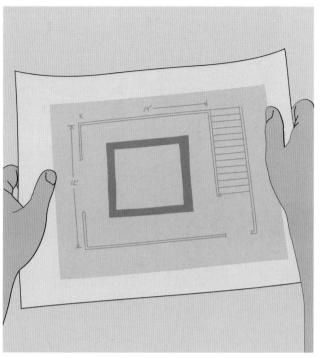

4 Place the transparency of the border over the room drawing. Move it around to find the best layout. Tape the border transparency in place over the room drawing. Draw perpendicular lines through the center of the border and calculate the distance from the center lines to the border.

5 Transfer the measurements from the border transparency onto your floor, starting with your center lines. Snap chalk lines to establish your layout for the border.

6 Lay out the border along the reference lines in a dry run. Do a dry run of the field tiles along the center lines inside and outside of the border. Make any adjustments, if necessary.

How to Lay a Running-bond Tile Pattern

1 Start running-bond tile by dry-fitting tile to establish working reference lines. Dry-fit a few tiles side by side using spacers. Measure the total width of the dry-fitted section (A). Use this measurement to snap a series of equally spaced parallel lines to help keep your tiles straight during installation. Running-bond layouts are most effective with rectangular tiles.

2 Starting at a point where the layout lines intersect, spread thin-set mortar and lay the first row of tiles. Offset the next row by a measurement that's equal to one-half the length of the tile plus one-half the width of the grout line.

3 Continue setting tiles, filling one quadrant at a time. Use the parallel reference lines as guides to keep the rows straight. Immediately wipe away any mortar that falls on the tiles. When finished, allow the mortar to cure, then grout and clean the tile (see pages 152 to 154).

How to Lay Hexagonal Tile

1 Snap perpendicular reference lines on the underlayment. Lay out three or four tiles in each direction along the layout lines. Place plastic spacers between the tiles to maintain even spacing. Measure the length of this layout in both directions (A and B). Use measurement A to snap a series of equally spaced parallel lines across the entire floor, then do the same for measurement B in the other direction.

2 Apply dry-set mortar and begin setting tile the same way as with square tile (pages 148 to 152). Apply mortar directly to the underside of any tiles that extend outside the mortar bed.

3 Continue setting the tiles, using the grid layout and spacers to keep the tiles aligned. Wipe off any mortar that falls onto the tile surface. When finished, allow the mortar to set, then apply grout between tiles (pages 152 to 154).

How to Lay a Diagonal Pattern with a Perpendicular Border

1 Follow steps 1 to 6 on pages 157 to 158 to plan your border lay out in the room. Dry-fit border tiles with spacers in the planned area. Make sure the border tiles are aligned with the reference lines. Dry-fit tiles at the outside corners of the border arrangement.

Adjust the tile positions as necessary to create a layout with minimal cutting. When the layout of the tiles is set, snap chalk lines around the border tiles and trace along the edges of the outside tiles. Install the border tiles.

2 Draw diagonal layout lines at a 45° angle to the perpendicular reference lines.

3 Use standard tile-setting techniques to set field tiles inside the border. Kneel on a wide board to distribute your weight if you need to work in a tiled area that has not cured overnight.

Outdoor Floors

Floors aren't restricted your home's interior. They're also one of the most important elements in your landscape. By serving as a background for the rest of your landscape, outdoor flooring visually sets the tone for the yard. Carefully chosen flooring transforms a yard into a series of living spaces for your "outdoor home."

By their nature, outdoor floors must withstand heavy use and the seasonal stress of the weather. You'll need to carefully select your flooring materials, keeping in mind the style and purpose of the area as well as the climate in your region.

Brick, stone, concrete, wood, and gravel can be used alone or in combination to create attractive, durable outdoor floors. Look for ways of repeating materials used elsewhere in your landscape or house. For example, if you have an attractive wood fence, use the same type of wood in a deck. If your home has a distinctive brick façade, repeat this element in your patio or walkway.

A well constructed base is crucial to the success of an outdoor floor. The quality of the base, which protects the floor from time- and weather-inflicted damage, determines the longevity of the floor.

Photo courtesy of Walker & Zanger, Inc.

The circular layout of the stone floor on the left blends with the stone walkway and stone walls to create the perfect outdoor retreat. Setting the tiles at an angle gave the above floor a decorative touch that enhances this alluring outdoor setting.

The cobblestone floor accentuates the historic motif of this estate and takes visitors back in time.

The projects on the following pages show a walkway constructed with different sized flagstone pavers and a floor composed of brick pavers. Just like an indoor floor, an outdoor floor requires a level surface to ensure a smooth, level finished floor.

Installing floors outdoors requires the same planning and attention to detail as any other type of floor project. Because these projects don't have the room perimeters of traditional floors, you'll need to mark the floor area using stakes and mason's string, making sure your corners are square. Your prep work consists of removing soil to a consistent depth within your staked-out area.

Before using stone, tile, or adhesives for your outdoor floor, check with the manufacturer to make sure the products can be used outside. Some flooring materials are for indoor use only.

These outdoor floors use different sizes and shapes of tile to match the styles and personalities of the homes. The floors at the top of the page feature consistent patterns throughout, while the floors above and to the right offer borders and a change in layout for more visual appeal.

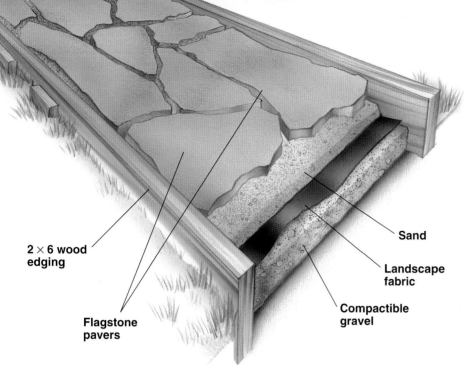

2 × 6 wood edging

Flagstone pavers

Sand

Landscape fabric

Compactible gravel

Flagstone Walkway

Natural flagstone is ideal for creating landscape floors. It's attractive and durable, and it blends well with formal and informal landscapes. Although flagstone structures are often mortared, they can be constructed using the sand-set method, which is faster and easier than mortar.

There are a variety of flat, thin sedimentary rocks that can be used for this project. Most home and garden stores carry flagstone, but stone supply yards usually have a greater variety. When buying flagstone, select pieces of all sizes. Arranging stones for the outdoor floor is similar to putting together a puzzle, and you need to see all of the pieces. Sort the stones by size, then spread them out to see each one.

Tools & Materials:

Rubber mallet, power drill, mason's string, stakes, tape measure, garden shovel, trenching spade, garden hose, hand tamp, circular saw with masonry blade, compactible gravel, landscape fabric, sand, 2 × 6 pressure-treated lumber, flagstone pavers.

How to Build a Flagstone Floor

1 Lay out the area with stakes and strings, and measure the diagonals to make sure it's square. Excavate the area 2" deeper than the thickness of the flagstone plus the depth of your compactible gravel base, and 3" outside of the string. Place 2 × 6 pressure-treated lumber under the strings. Drive stakes outside the edging, 12" apart, keeping the tops below ground level. Drive galvanized screws through the edging into the stakes.

2 Test-fit the stones, finding an attractive arrangement that limits the number of cuts needed. Gaps between stones should be ⅜" to 2" wide. Mark the stones for cutting, then set the stones aside in the same arrangement. Score along the marked lines with a circular saw and masonry blade set to ⅛" blade depth. Use a masonry chisel and hammer to strike along the scored line until the stone breaks.

3 Lay strips of landscape fabric over a base of compactible gravel, overlapping the strips by 6". Spread a 2" layer of sand over the fabric. Make a screed for smoothing the sand from a 2 × 6 that's notched to fit inside the edging. The depth of the notches should equal the thickness of the stones. Pull the screed across the floor, adding sand as needed to create a level base.

4 Beginning in a corner, lay the flagstones on the sand base, repeating the arrangement you created in Step 1 with ⅜" to 2" wide gaps between stones. If necessary, add or remove sand to level the stones, then set them by tapping them with a rubber mallet.

5 Fill the gaps between stones with sand. Pack sand into the gaps, then spray the entire walkway with water to help the sand settle. Continue packing sand until the gaps are completely filled.

Variation: Using the same technique for fitting and setting stones, you can easily create a flagstone patio.

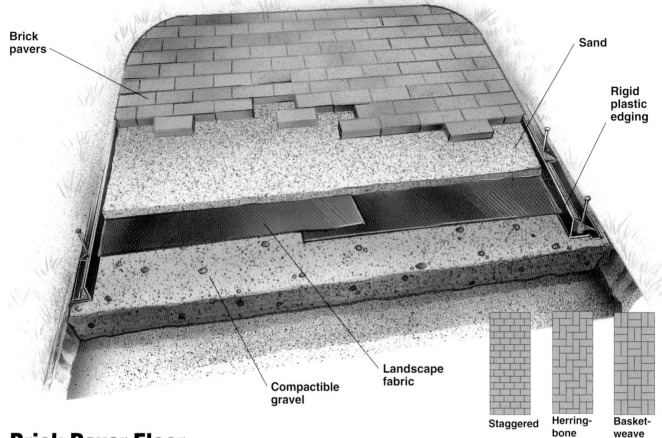

Brick pavers

Sand

Rigid plastic edging

Landscape fabric

Compactible gravel

Staggered   Herring-bone   Basket-weave

Brick Paver Floor

Brick pavers are versatile and durable, making them an excellent material for paving outdoor floors. They convey an impression of formality, quickly dressing up your landscape. Brick pavers are available in a variety of shapes, patterns, and colors to complement your landscape. It's best to use concrete pavers rather than traditional clay bricks. Concrete pavers have self-spacing lugs that make them easy to install.

The easiest way to build an outdoor floor with brick pavers is to set them in sand. With this method, the pavers rest on a 1" layer of sand spread over a prepared base. Pavers are then arranged over the sand, and the joints between them are densely packed with more sand. The sand helps keep the pavers in place, but it still allows them to shift as the ground contracts and expands with temperature changes.

Tools & Materials:

Rubber mallet, level, stakes, mason's string, tape measure, garden shovel, garden rake, trenching spade, garden hose, broom, hand tamp, circular saw with masonry blade, utility knife, landscape fabric, sand, 1"-thick pipes, galvanized spikes, brick pavers, compactible gravel, 2 × 4 lumber, plate compactor.

How to Build a Brick Paver Floor

1 Lay out the area with stakes and strings. Excavate 1" deeper than the thickness of the bricks plus the depth of the compactible gravel. Cut strips of landscape fabric. Lay them over a compactible gravel base, overlapping each strip 6". Install rigid plastic edging below the reference strings and drive galvanized spikes through the predrilled holes into the subbase. For rounded corners, use edging with notches on the outside flange. Remove the reference strings. Place 1"-thick pipes over the landscape fabric, spaced every 6 feet, for depth spacers.

2 Spread a 1" layer of sand over the landscape fabric, smoothing it with a garden rake to just cover the tops of the depth spacers. Water the sand thoroughly, then lightly pack it down with a hand tamp. Screed the sand to an even layer by resting a long 2 × 4 on the spacers and drawing it across the sand in a sawing motion. Fill footprints and low areas with sand, then water, tamp, and screed again. Remove the embedded spacers. Fill the grooves with sand and pack them smooth.

3 Lay the first border paver in a corner, placing it firmly against the plastic edging. Lay the next paver snug against the first. Set the pavers by tapping them into the sand with a mallet. Use the depth of the first paver as a guide for setting the remaining pavers in a 2-foot section. After each section is set, use a long level to make sure the pavers are flat. Make adjustments by tapping high pavers deeper into the sand or removing low pavers and adding a thin layer of sand.

4 Continue installing 2-foot sections of border and interior pavers. At rounded corners, install border pavers in a fan pattern with even gaps between pavers. Gentle curves may accommodate full-sized border pavers. For sharper bends, mark and cut wedge-shaped pavers to fit. Use a circular saw with masonry blade to make the cuts. Lay the remaining pavers. Use a 2 × 4 to check that the entire floor is level. Adjust any uneven pavers by tapping them with the mallet or adding more sand beneath them.

5 Spread a ½" layer of sand over the floor. Use a plate compactor to compress the entire floor and pack sand into the joints. Sweep up the loose sand, then soak the floor area thoroughly to settle the sand in the joints. Let the surface dry completely. If necessary, spread and pack sand over the floor again until all joints are tightly packed.

Carpet

Carpet remains one of the most popular and versatile of all floor coverings. Almost every home has wall-to-wall carpet in at least a few rooms. It's available in an almost endless variety of colors, styles, and patterns. It can also be custom made to express a more personal design. Most carpet is nylon based, although acrylic and polyester are also popular. Wool carpeting is more formal and more expensive, but also quite popular.

Part of carpet's appeal is its soft texture. It's pleasant to walk on—especially with bare feet, since it's soft and warm underfoot—and is comfortable for children to play on. Because carpet has a pad underneath that acts as a cushion, carpet can help reduce "floor fatigue."

Carpet absorbs more noise than most other floors, thereby reducing sound between rooms. It also serves as a natural insulator and decreases heat loss through the floor. Wall-to-wall carpet can increase the R-value, or insulation level, of a room.

Carpet offers several universal design advantages. With its non-skid surface, carpet helps reduce falls, which is important for people with limited mobility. Unlike some hard floors, carpet produces no glare, which helps people with vision limitations.

171

The warmth and comfort of carpet make it an ideal choice for the living room on the left and the bedroom above. The carpet in the living room invites a relaxing mood, while the bedroom carpet features a repeating, yet subtle, pattern for a luxurious look.

Carpet installation is significantly different than any other floor covering installation. Baseboards are left in place and the carpet is butted up tight against the trim rather than the trim being removed and placed on top of the finished floor. Carpet does not involve extensive subfloor preparation, and it doesn't require reference lines or drying time.

Nevertheless, installing carpet is a time-consuming job. Careful planning and layout are important to ensure the flow of carpet is continuous. You probably won't be able to cover your entire floor with one piece of carpet, so you'll end up with at least one seam. With an appropriate layout, you can keep the seams in low-traffic areas and make sure they remain invisible. If your carpet contains a pattern, the seams must be planned so the pattern runs uninterrupted.

Most installations require stretching the carpet with specialty tools in a carefully planned stretching sequence. Try laying carpet, stretching it, and matching seams on scrap pieces of plywood to hone your skills before starting the installation on your floor. As you gain confidence using the specialty tools and applying the installation techniques, the work becomes easier and faster.

You'll need a helper to carry the rolls of carpet, which can be quite heavy. You'll also need some assistance cutting the carpet to length. Once the carpet is roughly in place, you can finish the project on your own. For one-piece carpet installation in a room narrower than the carpet roll, such as a hallway, roll it out in a larger room or driveway and cut it, then loosely fold it lengthwise and bring it back into the project area.

Use the manufacturer's recommended pad under your carpet. Don't assume the free pad you receive with your carpet purchase is the correct one. If you're replacing old carpet, also replace the pad. The old one may contain mold and odors, and it's fairly inexpensive to replace.

Carpet can be installed over other floor covering, including hardwood. It can also be placed over concrete, provided the concrete is properly cured and you use a moisture barrier. Damp concrete will ruin carpet.

Make sure to order plenty of carpet so your purchase will come from the same dye lots. If you have to go back and buy more carpet, even if it's the same carpet from the same store and same manufacturer, there could be a minor variation in color.

Labels on the back of samples usually tell you the fiber composition, the available widths (usually 12 or 15 feet), what anti-stain treatments and other finishes were applied, and details of the product warranty.

Buying & Estimating Carpet

When choosing carpet, one thing to consider is color and pattern. Lighter shades and colors show dirt and stains more readily, but they provide an open, spacious feel. Darker colors and multi-colored patterns don't show as much dirt or wear, but they can also make a room appear smaller.

The materials used in a carpet and its construction can affect the carpet's durability. In high traffic areas, such as hallways and entryways, a top-quality fiber will last longer. Carpet construction, the way in which fibers are attached to the backing, impacts resistance to wear and appearance.

Available widths of certain carpets may affect your buying decision, because a roll that's wide enough to cover an entire room eliminates the need for seaming. When seaming is unavoidable, calculate the total square footage to be covered, then add 20 percent to cover trimming and seaming.

The type of carpet will dictate the type of pad you should use. Check carpet sample labels for the manufacturer's recommendations. Since carpet and padding work in tandem to create a floor covering system, use the best pad you can afford that works with your carpet. In addition to making your carpet feel more plush underfoot, the pad makes your floor quieter and warmer. A high-quality pad also helps reduce carpet wear.

Tips for Evaluating Carpet

Fiber Type	Characteristics
Nylon	Easy to clean, very durable, good stain resistance; colors sometimes fade in direct sunlight.
Polyester	Excellent stain resistance, very soft in thick cut-pile constructions; colors don't fade in sunlight.
Olefin	Virtually stain- and fade-proof, resists moisture and static; not as resilient as nylon or as soft as polyester.
Acrylic	Resembles wool in softness and look, good moisture resistance; less durable than other synthetics.
Wool	Luxurious look and feel, good durability and warmth; more costly and less stain-resistant than synthetics.

Consider fiber composition when selecting a carpet and choose materials with characteristics suited for your application.

Carpet Construction

The top surface of a carpet, called the *pile*, consists of yarn loops pushed up through a backing material. The loops are left intact or cut by the manufacturer, depending on the desired effect. Most carpet sold today is made from synthetic fibers, such as nylon, polyester, and olefin, although natural wool carpet is still popular.

A good rule of thumb for judging the quality of a carpet is to look at the pile density. Carpet with many pile fibers packed into a given area will resist crushing, repel stains and dirt buildup better, and be more durable than carpet with low pile density.

Cushion-backed carpet has a foam backing bonded to it, eliminating the need for additional padding. Cushion-backed carpet is easy to install because it doesn't require stretching or tackless strips. Instead, it's secured to the floor with general-purpose adhesive, much like full-spread sheet vinyl. Cushion-backed carpet usually costs less than conventional carpet, but it's generally a lower-quality product.

Loop-pile carpet has a textured look created by the rounded ends of the uncut yarn loops pushed up through the backing. The loops can be arranged randomly or they can make a distinct pattern, such as herringbone. Loop pile is ideal for heavy-traffic areas since loops are virtually impervious to crushing.

Velvet cut-pile carpet has the densest pile of any carpet type. It's cut so the color remains uniform when the pile is brushed in any direction. Velvets are well suited to formal living spaces.

Saxony cut-pile carpet, also known as plush, is constructed to withstand crushing and matting better than velvets. The pile is trimmed at a bevel, giving it a speckled appearance.

Cushion-backed

Loop-pile

Velvet cut-pile

Saxony cut-pile

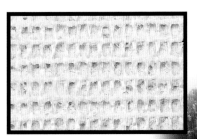

Examine the backing or "foundation" of the carpet. A tighter grid pattern (left) usually indicates dense-pile carpet that will be more durable and soil-resistant than carpet with looser pile (right).

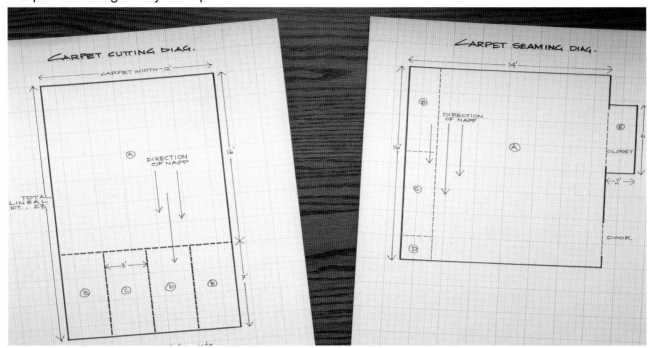

Sketch a scale drawing of the factory carpet roll and another drawing of the room to be carpeted. Use the drawings to plan the cuts and determine how the carpet pieces will be arranged. In most large rooms, the installation will include one large piece of carpet the same width as the factory roll and several smaller pieces that are permanently seamed to the larger piece. When sketching the layout, remember that carpet pieces must be oversized to allow for precise seaming and trimming. Your finished drawings will tell you the length of carpet you need to buy.

Keep pile direction consistent. Carpet pile is usually slanted, which affects how the carpet looks from different angles as light reflects off the surface. Place seamed pieces so the pile faces the same direction.

Maintain patterns when seaming patterned carpet. Because of this necessity, there's always more waste when installing patterned carpet. For a pattern that repeats itself every 18", for example, each piece must be oversized 18" to ensure the pattern is aligned. Pattern repeat measurements are noted on carpet samples.

At seams, add an extra 3" to each piece when estimating the amount of carpet you'll need. This extra material helps when cutting straight edges for seaming.

At each wall, add 6" for each edge that's along the wall. This surplus will be trimmed away when the carpet is cut to the exact size of the room.

Closet floors are usually covered with a separate piece of carpet that's seamed to the carpet in the main room area.

For stairs, add together the rise and run of each step to estimate the carpet needed for the stairway. Measure the width of the stairway to determine how many strips you can cut from the factory roll. For a 3 ft.-wide stairway, for example, you can cut three strips from a 12 ft.-wide roll, allowing for waste. Rather than seaming carpet strips together end to end, plan the installation so the ends of the strips fall in the stair crotches (see page 197). When possible, try to carpet stairs with a single carpet strip.

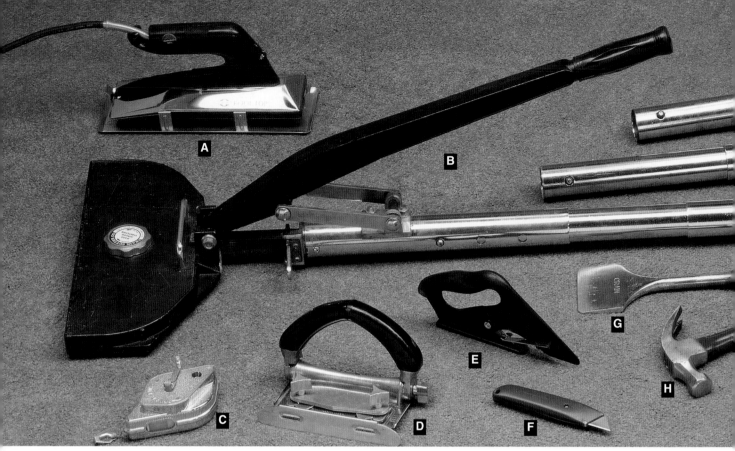

Carpeting tools include: seam iron (A), power stretcher and extensions (B), chalk line (C), edge trimmer (D), row-running knife (E), utility knife (F), stair tool (G), hammer (H), knee kicker (I), aviation snips (J), scissors (K), and stapler (L).

Tools & Materials for Installing Carpet

Installing carpet requires the use of some specialty tools, most notably the knee kicker and power stretcher. These tools are available at most rental centers and carpet stores.

Other than the carpet itself, the pad is the most important material in carpet installation. In addition to making your carpet feel more comfortable, it helps reduce sounds. The pad also helps keep warm air from escaping through your floor, thereby keeping the carpet warmer.

By cushioning the carpet fibers, the pad reduces wear and extends the life of your carpet. Be sure to use a quality pad.

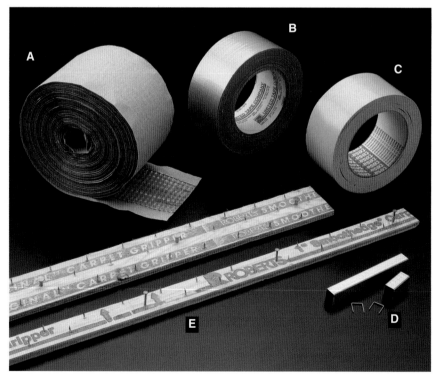

Carpeting materials include: hot-glue seam tape (A), used to join carpet pieces together; duct tape (B), for seaming carpet pads; double-sided tape (C), used to secure carpet pads to concrete; staples (D), used to fasten padding to underlayment; and tackless strips (E), for securing the edges of stretched carpet.

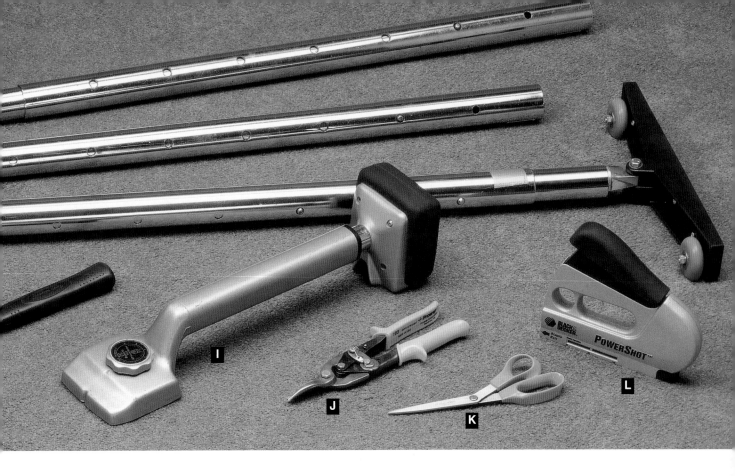

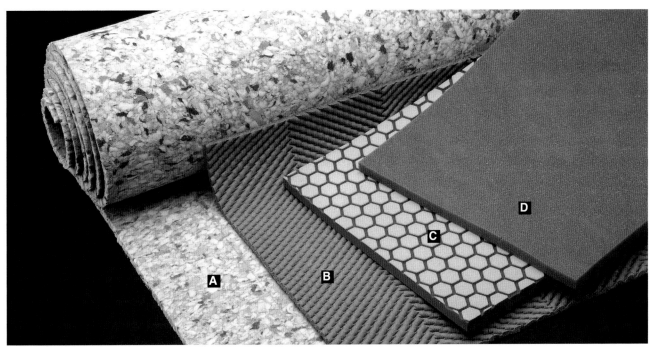

Carpet padding comes in several varieties, including: bonded urethane foam (A), cellular sponge rubber (B), grafted prime foam (C), and prime urethane (D). Bonded urethane padding is suitable for low-traffic areas, while prime urethane and grafted prime foam are better for high-traffic areas. In general, cut pile, cut-and-loop, and high-level loop carpets perform best with prime or bonded urethane or rubber pads that are less than 7/16" thick. For berbers or other stiff-backed carpets, use 3/8"-thick bonded urethane foam or cellular sponge rubber. Foam padding is graded by density: the denser the foam, the better the pad. Rubber padding is graded by weight: the heavier, the better.

Using Carpet Tools

The knee kicker and power stretcher are the two most important tools for installing carpet. They are used to stretch a carpet smooth and taut before securing it to tackless strips installed around the perimeter of a room.

The power stretcher is the more efficient of the two tools and should be used to stretch and secure as much of the carpet as possible. The knee kicker is used to secure carpet in tight areas where the power stretcher can't reach, such as closets.

A logical stretching sequence is essential to good carpet installation. Begin by attaching the carpet at a doorway or corner, then use the power stretcher and knee kicker to stretch the carpet away from the attached areas and toward the opposite walls.

Using a Knee Kicker

Shown cut away for clarity

1 A knee kicker (and power stretcher) has teeth that grab the carpet foundation for stretching. Adjust the depth of the teeth by turning the knob on the knee kicker head. The teeth should be set deep enough to grab the carpet foundation without penetrating to the padding.

2 Place the kicker head a few inches away from the wall to avoid dislodging the tackless strips, then strike the kicker cushion firmly with your knee, stretching the carpet taut. Tack the carpet to the pins on the tackless strips to hold it in place.

Using a Power Stretcher

Tail   **Extension poles**   **Head**

1 Align the pieces of the power stretcher along the floor with the tail positioned at a point where the carpet is already secured and the head positioned just short of the opposite wall. Fit the ends of the sections together.

2 Telescope one or more of the extension poles until the tail rests against the starting wall or block and the head is about 5" from the opposite wall.

3 Adjust the teeth on the head so they grip the carpet foundation (see step 1, opposite page). Depress the lever on the head to stretch the carpet. The stretcher head should move the carpet about 2".

Installing Carpet Transitions

Metal carpet bar

Tackless strip tuck-under

Hot-glue seam tape

Hardwood threshold

Doorways, entryways, and other transition areas require special treatment when installing carpet. Transition materials and techniques vary, depending on the level and type of the adjoining flooring (see photos, left).

For a transition to a floor that's either at the same height or lower than the bottom of the carpet, attach a metal carpet bar to the floor and secure the carpet inside the bar. This transition is often used where carpet meets a vinyl or tile floor. Carpet bars are sold in standard door-width lengths and in longer strips.

For a transition to a floor that's higher than the carpet bottom, use tackless strips, as if the adjoining floor surface was a wall. This transition is common where carpet meets a hardwood floor.

For a transition to another carpet of the same height, join the two carpet sections together with hot-glue seam tape.

For a transition in a doorway between carpets of different heights or textures, install tackless strips and a hardwood threshold. Thresholds are available predrilled and ready to install with screws.

Tools & Materials:

Hacksaw, marker, utility knife, knee kicker, stair tool, straight-edge, screwdriver, transition materials, wood block.

How to Make Transitions with Metal Carpet Bars

1 Measure and cut a carpet bar to fit the threshold, using a hacksaw. Nail the carpet bar in place. In doorways, the upturned metal flange should lie directly under the center of the door when it's closed.

2 Roll out, cut, and seam the carpet. Fold the carpet back in the transition area, then mark it for trimming. The edge of the carpet should fall ⅛" to ¼" short of the corner of the carpet bar so it can be stretched into the bar.

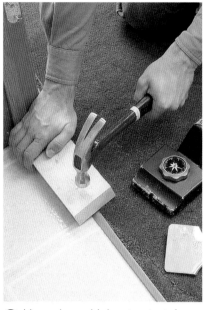

3 Use a knee kicker to stretch the carpet snugly into the corner of the carpet bar. Press the carpet down onto the pins with a stair tool. Bend the carpet bar flange down over the carpet by striking it with a hammer and a block of wood.

How to Make Transitions with Tackless Strips

1 Install a tackless strip, leaving a gap equal to ⅔ the thickness of the carpet for trimming. Roll out, cut, and seam the carpet. Mark the edge of the carpet between the tackless strip and the adjoining floor surface about ⅛" past the point where it meets the adjacent floor.

2 Use a straightedge and utility knife to trim the excess carpet. Stretch the carpet toward the strip with a knee kicker, then press it onto the pins of the tackless strip.

3 Tuck the edge of the carpet into the gap between the tackless strip and the existing floor, using a stair tool.

Installing Padding & Tackless Strips

The easiest way to secure carpeting is to install tackless strips around the perimeter of the room. Once the strips are installed, carpet padding is rolled out as a foundation for the carpet.

Standard ¾"-wide tackless strips are adequate for securing most carpet. For carpets laid on concrete, use wider tackless strips that are attached to the concrete with masonry nails. Be careful when handling the tackless strips, since the sharp pins can be dangerous. Where the carpet meets a doorway or another type of flooring, install the appropriate transitions (see pages 182 to 183).

Tools & Materials:

Aviation snips, utility knife, hammer, stapler, tackless strips, nails, carpet pad, duct tape.

How to Install Tackless Strips

1 Starting in a corner, nail tackless strips to the floor, keeping a gap between the strips and the walls that's about ⅔ the thickness of the carpet. Use plywood spacers. Angled pins on the strip should point toward the wall.

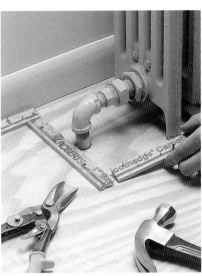

2 Use aviation snips to cut tackless strips to fit around radiators, door moldings, and other obstacles.

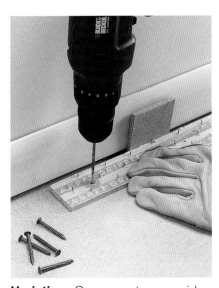

Variation: On concrete, use wider tackless strips. Drill pilot holes through the strips and into the floor, using a masonry bit, then fasten the strips by driving 1½" fluted masonry nails.

How to Install Carpet Padding

1 Roll out enough padding to cover the entire floor. Make sure the seams between the padding are tight. If one face of the padding has a slicker surface, keep the slick surface face up, making it easier to slide the carpet over the pad during installation.

2 Use a utility knife to cut away excess padding along the edges. The padding should touch, but not overlap, the tackless strips.

3 Tape the seams together with duct tape, then staple the padding to the floor every 12".

Variation: To fasten padding to a concrete floor, apply double-sided tape next to the tackless strips, along the seams, and in an "X" pattern across the floor.

How to Cut & Seam Carpet

1 Position the carpet roll against one wall, with its loose end extending up the wall about 6", then roll out the carpet until it reaches the opposite wall.

2 At the opposite wall, mark the back of the carpet at each edge about 6" beyond the point where the carpet touches the wall. Pull the carpet back away from the wall so the marks are visible.

Variation: When cutting loop-pile carpet, avoid severing the loops by cutting it from the top side, using a row-running knife. Fold the carpet back along the cut line to part the pile (left) and make a crease along the part line. Lay the carpet flat and cut along the part in the pile (right). Cut slowly to ensure a smooth, straight cut.

3 Snap a chalk line across the back of the carpet between the marks. Place a scrap piece of plywood under the cutting area to protect the carpet and padding from the knife blade. Cut along the line, using a straightedge and utility knife.

4 Next to walls, straddle the edge of the carpet and nudge it with your foot until it extends up the wall by about 6" and is parallel to the wall.

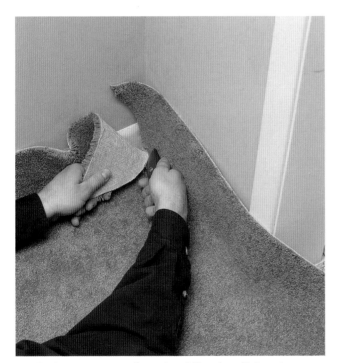

5 At the corners, relieve buckling by slitting the carpet with a utility knife, allowing the carpet to lie somewhat flat. Make sure that corner cuts do not cut into usable carpet.

6 Using your seaming plan (see page 176) as a guide, measure and cut fill-in pieces of carpet to complete the installation. Be sure to include a 6" surplus at each wall and a 3" surplus on each edge that will be seamed to another piece of carpet. Set the cut pieces in place, making sure the pile faces in the same direction on all pieces.

(continued next page)

7 Roll back the large piece of carpet on the side to be seamed, then use a chalk line to snap a straight seam edge about 2" from the factory edge. Keep the ends of the line about 18" from the sides of the carpet where the overlap onto the walls causes the carpet to buckle.

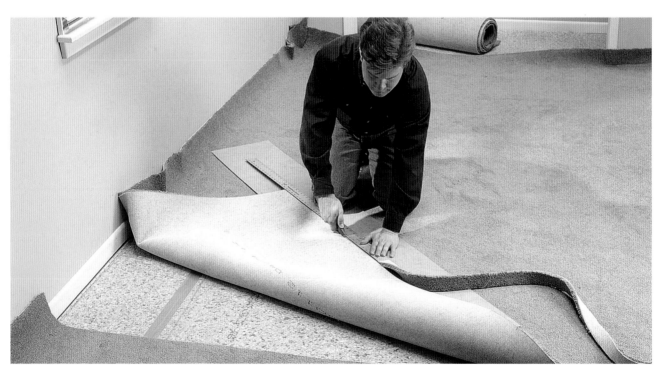

8 Using a straightedge and utility knife, carefully cut the carpet along the chalk line. To extend the cutting lines to the edges of the carpet, pull the corners back at an angle so they lie flat, then cut the line with the straightedge and utility knife. Place scrap wood under the cutting area to protect the carpet while cutting.

9 On smaller carpet pieces, cut straight seam edges where the small pieces will be joined to one another. Don't cut the edges that will be seamed to the large carpet piece until after the small pieces are joined together.

Option: Apply a continuous bead of seam glue along the cut edges of the backing at seams to ensure that the carpet will not fray.

10 Plug in the seam iron and set it aside to heat up, then measure and cut hot-glue seam tape for all seams. Begin by joining the small fill-in pieces to form one large piece. Center the tape under the seam with the adhesive side facing up.

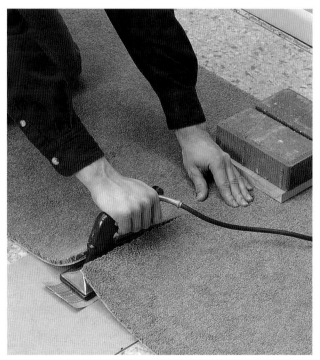

11 Set the iron under the carpet at one end of the tape until the adhesive liquifies, usually about 30 seconds. Working in 12" sections, slowly move the iron along the tape, letting the carpet fall onto the hot adhesive behind it. Set weights at the end of the seam to hold the pieces in place.

(continued next page)

12 Press the edges of the carpet together into the melted adhesive behind the iron. Separate the pile with your fingers to make sure no fibers are stuck in the glue and the seam is tight, then place a weighted board over the seam to keep it flat while the glue sets.

Variation: To close any gaps in loop-pile carpet seams, use a knee kicker to gently push the seam edges together while the adhesive is still hot.

13 Continue seaming the fill-in pieces together. When the tape adhesive has dried, turn the seamed piece over and cut a fresh seam edge as done in steps 7 and 8. Reheat and remove about 1½" of tape from the end of each seam to keep it from overlapping the tape on the large piece.

14 Use hot-glue seam tape to join the seamed pieces to the large piece of carpet, repeating steps 10 through 12.

15 If you're laying carpet in a closet, cut a fill-in piece and join it to the main carpet with hot-glue seam tape.

Tip: At radiators, pipes, and other obstructions, cut slits in the carpet with a utility knife. Cut long slits from the edge of the carpet to the obstruction, then cut short cross-slits where the carpet will fit around the obstruction.

Tip: To fit carpet around partition walls where the edges of the wall or door jamb meet the floor, make diagonal cuts from the edge of the carpet at the center of the wall to the points where the edges of the wall meet the floor.

How to Stretch & Secure Carpet

1 Before stretching the seamed carpet, read through this entire section and create a stretching sequence similar to the one shown here. Start by fastening the carpet at a doorway threshold using carpet transitions (see pages 182 to 183).

2 If the doorway is close to a corner, use the knee kicker to secure the carpet to the tackless strips between the door and the corner. Also secure a few feet of carpet along the adjacent wall, working toward the corner.

3 Use a power stretcher to stretch the carpet toward the wall opposite the door. Brace the tail with a length of 2 × 4 placed across the doorway. Leaving the tail in place and moving only the stretcher head, continue stretching and securing the carpet along the wall, working toward the nearest corner in 12" to 24" increments.

4 As you stretch the carpet, secure it onto the tackless strips with a stair tool and hammer.

5 With the power stretcher still extended from the doorway to the opposite side of the room, knee-kick the carpet onto the tackless strips along the closest wall, starting near the corner closest to the stretcher tail. Disengage and move the stretcher only if it's in the way.

6 Reposition the stretcher so its tail is against the center of the wall you just secured. Stretch and secure the carpet along the opposite wall, working from the center toward a corner. If there's a closet in an adjacent wall, work toward that wall, not the closet.

(continued next page)

How to Stretch & Secure Carpet (continued)

7 Use the knee kicker to stretch and secure the carpet inside the closet (if any). Stretch and fasten the carpet against the back wall first, then do the side walls. After the carpet in the closet is stretched and secured, use the knee kicker to secure the carpet along the walls next to the closet. Disengage the power stretcher only if it's in the way.

8 Return the head of the power stretcher to the center of the wall. Finish securing carpet along this wall, working toward the other corner of the room.

9 Reposition the stretcher to secure the carpet along the last wall of the room, working from the center toward the corners. The tail block should be braced against the opposite wall.

Tip: Locate any floor vents under the stretched carpet, then use a utility knife to cut away the carpet, starting at the center. It's important that this be done only after the stretching is complete.

10 Use a carpet edge trimmer to trim surplus carpet away from the walls. At corners, use a utility knife to finish the cuts.

11 Tuck the trimmed edges of the carpet neatly into the gaps between the tackless strips and the walls, using a stair tool and hammer.

Stair riser

Tackless strips

Stair tread

On stairways, tackless strips are attached to the treads and risers. Where two or more pieces of carpet are needed, the pieces should meet at the "crotch" of the step, where the riser and tread meet.

Basic Techniques for Carpeting Stairs

Where practical, try to carpet stairs with a single strip of carpet. If you must use two or more pieces, plan the layout so the pieces meet where a riser meets a tread. Do not seam carpet pieces together in the middle of a tread or riser.

The project shown here involves a staircase that's enclosed on both sides. For open staircases, turn down the edges of the carpet and secure them with carpet tacks.

Tools & Materials:

Straightedge, utility knife, aviation snips, stapler, stair tool, knee kicker, carpet, carpet padding, tackless strips, nails.

How to Carpet Stairs

1 Measure the width of the stairway. Add together the vertical rise and horizontal run of the steps to determine how much carpet you'll need. Use a straightedge and utility knife to carefully cut the carpet to the correct dimensions.

2 Fasten tackless strips to the risers and the treads. On the risers, place the strips about 1" above the treads. On the treads, place the strips about ¾" from the risers. Make sure the pins point toward the crotch of the step. On the bottom riser, leave a gap equal to ⅔ the carpet thickness.

196

3 For each step, cut a piece of carpet padding the width of the step and long enough to cover the tread and a few inches of the riser below it. Staple the padding in place.

4 Position the carpet on the stairs with the pile direction pointing down. Secure the bottom edge using a stair tool to tuck the end of the carpet between the tackless strip and the floor.

5 Use a knee kicker and stair tool to stretch the carpet onto the tackless strip on the first tread. Start in the center of the step, then alternate kicks on either side until the carpet is completely secured on the step.

6 Use a hammer and stair tool to wedge the carpet firmly into the back corner of the step. Repeat this process for each step.

7 Where two carpet pieces meet, secure the edge of the upper piece first, then stretch and secure the lower piece.

Floor Finishes

One of the most desirable features of hardwood flooring is that it's a natural product. The grain patterns are interesting to the eye and the combination of colors gives any room a soft, inviting glow. The resilience of wood fibers makes a hardwood floor extremely durable, but they are susceptible to changes caused by moisture and aging.

Typically, the first thing to wear out on a hardwood floor is the finish. Refinishing the floor by sanding it with a rented drum sander and applying a topcoat, such as polyurethane, will make your old floor look new. If you don't want to sand the floor, but want to retain the floor's aged glow, or if the boards have been sanded before and are less than ⅜" thick, consider stripping the floor.

Once your floor is finished, you may want to dress it up with a favorite design, border, or pattern. If the wood will not look good refinished, consider painting it. Pages 204 to 223 offer exciting ways to customize your wood floor.

Resurfacing & Refinishing Supplies

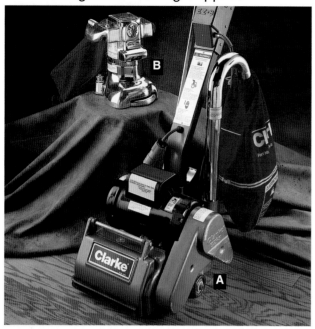

Specialty tools and products are necessary for resurfacing or refinishing wood floors. If several scratches, gouges, and stains have damaged the floor, it may be a good idea to resurface it by sanding, using a drum sander (A) for the main floor area and an edger sander (B) for areas next to baseboards. Both tools can be rented from home improvement or rental centers. As a general rule, use the finest-grit sandpaper that's effective for the job. Be sure to get complete operating and safety instructions when renting these tools.

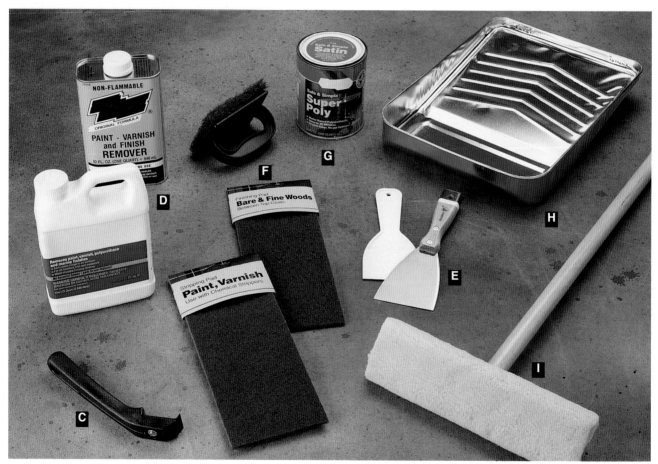

Other products and tools for resurfacing and refinishing floors: Paint scrapers (C) are helpful for removing old finish in corners and other areas that cannot be reached by sanders. When refinishing floors, chemical stripping products (D) are often a more efficient method that yields better results. This is especially true for floors that are uneven, or for parquet and veneered floors, which cannot be sanded. Stripper knives (E) and abrasive pads (F) are used with the stripping products. For the final finish, water-based polyurethane (G) is poured into a paint tray (H) and applied using a wide painting pad with a pole extension (I).

How to Refinish a Hardwood Floor

1 Using 80-grit sandpaper, position the drum sander about 6" from the wall. With the drum raised, start the machine and move it forward, slowly lowering the drum. Sand in the direction of the floorboards, to within 12" of the end wall, and raise the drum with the sander in motion.

2 Return to your starting point and begin the second pass, overlapping the first path by one-half its width.

3 The first stage of sanding should remove most of the old finish. Then switch to a 120-grit sandpaper and resand the entire floor. Repeat the sanding process, using finer sandpaper, 150- to 180-grit, to remove scratches left by the coarser papers.

4 Sand along the edges with an edger using the same sequence of sandpapers used with the drum sander.

5 Use a scraper to scrape old finish from hard-to-reach areas. Hand-sand the area smooth.

6 Wipe the floor with a tack cloth to remove dust, and apply the topcoat of your choice. Polyurethane is a good product for a clear, durable finish.

How to Apply Polyurethane to Floors

1 Seal the sanded wood with a 1:1 mixture of water-based polyurethane and water, using a painting pad and pole. Allow the floor to dry, then buff the surface lightly to remove any raised wood grain, using a medium abrasive pad. Vacuum the surface, using a bristle attachment, then wipe with a tack cloth.

2 Apply a coat of undiluted polyurethane to the floor. Apply the finish as evenly as possible. Do not overbrush. Allow the finish to dry before continuing.

3 Buff the floor with a medium abrasive pad. Vacuum the floor, then wipe it with a tack cloth. Apply more coats of polyurethane as needed to build the finish to a desired thickness, buffing between coats. Most floors require at least three coats of water-based polyurethane for a hard, durable finish.

Option: When the final coat of finish is dry, buff the surface with water and a fine abrasive pad to remove any surface imperfections and diminish gloss.

How to Chemically Strip a Hardwood Floor

1 Wearing a respirator and rubber gloves, apply the stripper with a paintbrush. Cover only an area small enough to be scraped within the working time of the stripper.

2 Scrape off the sludge of stripper and old finish, using a nylon stripper knife. Move the scraper with the wood grain, and deposit the sludge onto old newspapers. After the entire floor is stripped, scrub it with an abrasive pad dipped in a rinsing solvent, such as mineral spirits, that's compatible with your stripping product. Do not use water.

3 Clean residual sludge and dirt from the joints between floorboards, using a palette knife or putty knife.

4 Remove stains and discoloration by carefully sanding only the affected area. Use oxalic acid on deep stains.

5 Touch up sanded areas with wood stain. Test the stain before applying.

Applying Wood Stain & Aged & Distressed Finishes

Stains are applied to surfaces of unfinished wood floors to change the color and are available in a variety of natural wood tones. Colored stains can be applied to previously stained and finished floors for a colorwashed effect. Consider a colored stain, such as green for a rustic decorating scheme, or white for a contemporary look.

You can stain wood by colorwashing it with diluted latex paint. The colorwash solution will be considerably lighter in color than the original paint color. Use 1 part latex paint and 4 parts water to make a colorwash solution, and experiment with small amounts of paint until you achieve the desired color. Apply the stain or colorwash solution in an inconspicuous area, such as a closet, to test the application method and color before staining the entire floor surface.

Aged finishes (see page 207) give floors time-worn character, making them especially suitable for a rustic or transitional decorating style. Although they appear distressed and fragile, these finishes are actually very durable. Aged finishes

are especially suitable on previously painted or stained floors, but they may also be applied to new or resurfaced wood flooring. Up to three coats of paint in different colors may be used.

Look for a water-based stain that's formulated for easy application without lap marks or streaking. Conditioners can help prevent streaking and control grain raise when you're using water-based wood stains. Use a wood conditioner on the wood prior to staining, if recommended by the manufacturer.

Tools & Materials:

Synthetic brush, sponge applicators, cotton lint-free rags, rubber gloves, paint pad and pole extension, power sander, fine- and medium-grit sandpaper, vacuum, wood conditioner, tack cloth, water-based stain or latex paint, high-gloss and satin clear finishes, latex enamel paints, paint roller, hammer, chisel, awl.

How to Apply a Stained Finish to a Bare Wood Floor

1 Sand the floor surface, using fine-grit sandpaper, sanding in the direction of the wood grain. Remove the sanding dust with a vacuum, then wipe the floor with a tack cloth.

2 Wear rubber gloves when working with any stain product. Stir the stain or colorwash solution thoroughly. Apply the stain or solution to the floor, using a synthetic brush or sponge applicator. Work on one small section at a time. Keep a wet edge and avoid overlapping the brush strokes.

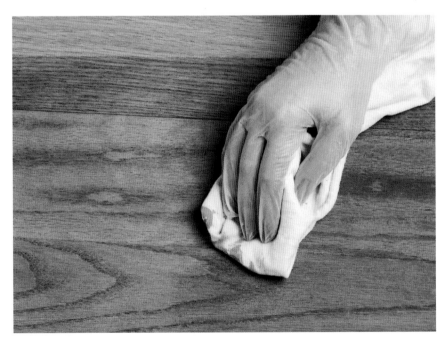

3 Wipe away excess stain immediately, or after the waiting time recommended by the manufacturer, using a dry, lint-free rag. Wipe across the grain of the wood first, then wipe with the grain. Continue applying and wiping stain until the entire floor is finished. Allow the stain to dry. Sand the floor lightly, using fine-grit sandpaper, then remove any sanding dust with a tack cloth. For a deeper color, apply a second coat of stain and allow it to dry thoroughly.

4 Apply a coat of high-gloss clear finish to the stained floor, using a sponge applicator or a paint pad with pole extension. Allow the finish to dry. Sand the floor lightly, using fine-grit sandpaper, then wipe with a tack cloth. Apply two coats of satin clear finish following manufacturer's directions.

Dark wood tones work well for traditional rooms. White color-washing over a previously dark stained floor mellows the formal appearance.

Medium, warm wood tones have a casual appearance. White color-washing over a medium wood tone creates an antiqued look.

Pale neutral stains often are used for contemporary rooms. A blue colorwash can give a pale floor a bold new character.

How to Apply an Aged & Distressed Finish

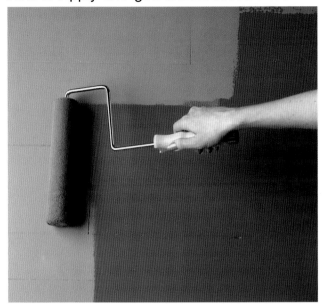

1 Finish the floor with a painted or stained base coat. Sand the floor lightly, using fine-grit sandpaper. Vacuum the floor and wipe away dust with a tack cloth. Apply two or three coats of enamel, using a different color of paint for each coat. Allow the floor to dry between coats. Sand the floor lightly between coats, using fine-grit sandpaper, and wipe away dust with a tack cloth.

2 Sand the floor surface with medium-grit sandpaper, sanding harder in some areas to remove the top and middle coats of paint, using a power sander. Avoid sanding beyond the base coat of paint or stain.

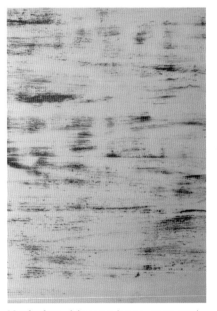

3 To distress the floor further, hit the wood with the head of a hammer or a chain. Gouge the boards with a chisel, or pound holes randomly, using an awl. Create as many imperfections as desired, then sand the floor lightly with fine-grit sandpaper. Apply two coats of satin clear finish, allowing the floor to dry completely between coats.

Variation: Two coats of dark green paint were applied over a previously stained floor. Sanding revealed the stain in some areas. The floor was further distressed, using a hammer, chisel, and awl.

Variation: Maroon base coat and light rose top coat were painted over a previously stained floor. Sanding created an aged look suitable for a cottage bedroom.

Creating a Painted Checkerboard Floor Design

Painted designs in a variety of styles can be applied to wood floors to give the entire floor a new look or to accent certain areas. If the floor is in poor condition, it can be camouflaged with an all-over design, such as a classic checkerboard pattern.

Proper preparation of the floor is essential to give long-lasting results. For a previously finished wood floor, lightly sand the areas to be painted so the paint will adhere well to the finish. For an unfinished wood floor, prevent the paint from penetrating the grain of the bare wood by sealing it with a clear acrylic or polyurethane finish and sanding it lightly before it's painted. Be sure the floor is free of dust before you start to paint.

Choose colors that complement each other for an attractive finish. A dark color against a light color provides a good contrast. You may want to apply the paints to a small area of inconspicu-ous flooring, such as a closet, to see how they look together before painting the entire floor.

Express your creativity by making a custom floor cloth with decorative painting, featured on page 211. Used at the entryway to the living room or as an area rug, a floor cloth can become a conversation piece.

Tools & Materials:

Power sander with fine-grit sandpaper, paintbrushes, tape measure, straightedge, pencil, paint roller or paint pad and pole extension, graph paper, tack cloth, putty knife, painter's masking tape, latex paint in the two desired colors and sheen, high-gloss and satin clear finishes.

For the decorative floor cloth include: synthetic-bristle paintbrush, plastic drop cloth, carpenter's square, 18-oz or #8 canvas, sealer.

How to Paint a Checkerboard Design on a Wood Floor

1 Degloss the finish of a previously stained and sealed wood floor by sanding the surface lightly, using a power sander and fine-grit sandpaper. This improves the paint adhesion. Vacuum the entire floor, then wipe it with a tack cloth to remove all sanding dust.

2 Mask off the baseboards with painter's masking tape. Paint the entire floor with the lighter of the two paint colors. Allow the paint to dry thoroughly.

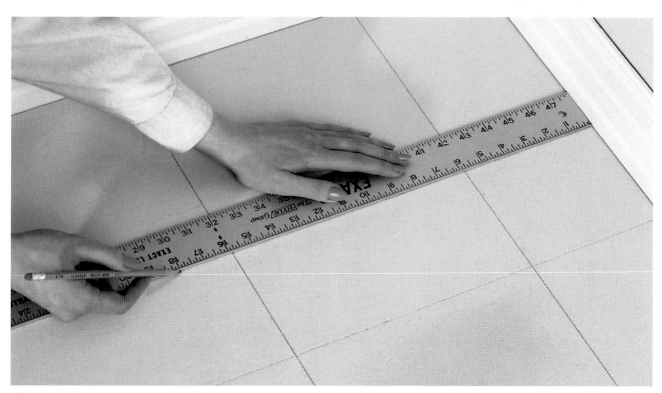

3 Measure the floor and determine the size of squares you'll use. Plan the design so the areas of the floor with the highest visibility, such as the main entrance, have full squares. Place partial squares along walls in less conspicuous areas. Mark the design lines on the floor, using a straightedge and pencil.

(continued next page)

4 Mask off the squares that are to remain light in color, using painter's masking tape. Press firmly along all edges of the tape, using a putty knife, to create a tight seal.

5 Paint the remaining squares with the darker paint color. Paint in small areas at a time, and remove the masking tape from painted squares before the paint is completely dry.

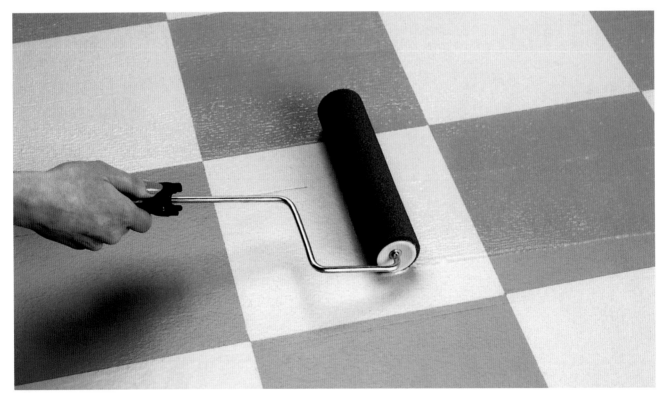

6 After all of the paint has dried completely, apply a coat of high-gloss clear finish, using a paint roller or a paint pad with pole extension. Allow the finish to dry. Sand the finish lightly with fine-grit sandpaper, then wipe the floor with a tack cloth. Apply two coats of satin clear finish.

How to Make a Painted Floor Cloth

1 Trim selvages from the canvas. Mark the canvas to the desired size, using a pencil, carpenter's square, and straightedge. Cut the canvas to size.

2 Machine stitch around the canvas ¼" from raw edges. Stitch a second row of stitching ⅛" from raw edges. Press the canvas so it lies flat.

3 Place the canvas on a plastic drop cloth. Using a paint roller, apply the background paint color, taking care not to crease the canvas. Roll the paint in all directions to penetrate the fabric. Allow it to dry. Apply additional coats of paint as necessary, allowing the paint to dry overnight. Trim any loose threads.

4 Mark your design, using a pencil. Paint the design, applying one color at a time. Use a fine-pointed brush for outlining and a wider brush for filling in the design areas. Allow the paint to dry 24 hours.

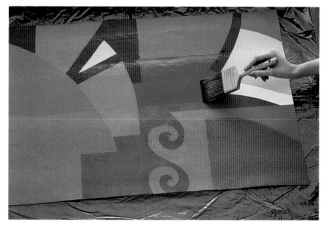

5 Apply sealer, using a synthetic-bristle paintbrush. Allow the sealer to dry for several hours. Apply two additional coats of sealer, following the manufacturer's instructions for drying time.

6 Place the canvas on the floor, making sure it lies perfectly flat.

Creating Faux Stone Floor Tile Designs

A painted finish that mimics unpolished stone can be applied to a floor using a stippler or pieces of newspaper. The stippling technique results in a relatively smooth textured finish with blended colors, while the newspaper method creates an unpolished stone finish with depth, color variation, and a rough visual texture. Adding rustic grout lines creates the look of expensive stone tiles.

A variety of earth-tone glazes can be combined to make a stone finish in the desired color. It's best to limit your selection to two or three colors.

To create grout lines, apply masking tape to the surface in a grid pattern before applying the faux finish. Once the finish has been applied and is dry, remove the tape and paint the lines with a rounded artist's brush. You can get a rustic look by painting the lines by hand or create the illusion of depth by "shadowing" the grout lines with a marker that's darker than the base coat color.

For faux stone flat glazes, mix one part latex paint, one part latex paint conditioner, and one part water for each shade of earth-toned flat glaze. For faux stone washes, mix one part flat latex paint and two to three parts water for each shade of wash. Dilute the paint with water until it reaches the consistency of ink.

Tools & Materials:

Low-napped roller, sponge applicator or paintbrush, stippler or newspaper, white low-luster latex enamel paint, flat latex paint in two or three earth-tone shades, latex paint conditioner, cheesecloth, flat latex paint in white and an earth-tone shade, matte clear finish or aerosol, matte clear acrylic sealer (optional), latex or craft acrylic paint in shade to contrast with stone finish.

How to Apply a Faux Stone Finish Using the Stippling Method

1 Apply a base coat of white low-luster latex enamel to the surface, using an applicator suitable to the surface size. Allow the paint to dry. Mask off grout lines, if desired.

2 Apply a flat earth-tone glaze in random strokes, using a sponge applicator or paintbrush. Cover about half of the surface. Repeat the random strokes with another color glaze in the remaining areas, leaving some small areas of the base coat unglazed.

3 Using a stippler, lightly brush over the surface. Blend the colors as desired, leaving some areas very dark and others light enough for the base coat to show through. Add white and black glazes, or earth-tone glazes, as desired. Blend the colors with the stippler, then allow the paint to dry.

4 Apply a white wash to the entire surface. Dab with a wadded cheesecloth to soften the finish. Allow the paint to dry, then apply matte clear finish or matte aerosol clear acrylic sealer, if desired.

How to Apply a Faux Stone Finish Using the Newspaper Method

1 Follow steps 1 and 2 on page 213. Apply a white wash in desired areas, and apply an earth-tone wash in other areas.

2 Fold a sheet of newspaper to several layers. Lay it flat over one area of the surface and press it into the glaze. Lift the paper, removing some of the glaze. Repeat in other areas, using the same newspaper, turning it in different directions to blend the colors roughly.

3 Add more color to an area by spreading glaze onto the newspaper and laying it flat on the surface. Repeat as necessary until the desired effect is achieved. Leave some dark accent areas in the finish as well as an occasional light spot. Use the same newspaper throughout. Allow the paint to dry.

4 Apply a white wash to the entire surface. Dab with a wadded cheesecloth to soften the colors. Allow the paint to dry, then apply a matte clear finish or matte aerosol clear acrylic sealer, if desired.

How to Apply Rustic Grout Lines

1 Apply a base coat of white low-luster latex enamel to the surface, using an applicator suitable to the surface size. Allow the paint to dry. Plan the placement of the grout lines, and mark the points of intersection, using a pencil and straightedge.

2 Stretch ¼" masking tape taut, and apply it to the surface in horizontal lines, positioning the tape lines just under the marked points. Repeat this process for the vertical lines, positioning the tape just right of the marks. Press the tape firmly in place with your fingers, but don't burnish the tape.

3 Apply the desired faux finish (pages 213-214). Allow the finish to dry, then carefully remove the tape lines.

4 Paint over the grout lines freehand, using a round artist's brush and a grout line glaze in a color that contrasts pleasingly with the faux finish. Allow the lines to have some irregularity in thickness and density. Allow the paint to dry. Apply a finish or sealer to the entire surface, as desired.

Applying Faux Wood Grain Floor Finish

The rich patterns and colors of natural wood grain can be imitated using a technique that dates back as far as Roman times and was especially popular in the late nineteenth century. Long revered as a technique used exclusively by skilled artisans, wood graining has made a recent comeback as new tools, such as the wood-graining rocker, have become available. Wood graining is a suitable finish for any smooth surface.

For faux wood grain, a glaze of thickened paint is applied over a base coat of low-luster latex enamel. The rocker side of a wood-graining tool is dragged through the wet glaze as the tool is rocked back and forth. The simultaneous dragging and rocking of the tool creates oval-shaped markings that simulate the characteristic grain of pine and other woods.

Become familiar with the graining technique by practicing it on a large sheet of cardboard until you can achieve a realistic look. This will also allow you to test the finish before applying it to the actual project.

The final color of the wood grain finish depends on the combined effect of the base coat and glaze coat. For an appearance of natural wood, use a lighter base coat and overlay it with a darker glaze. Because of the wide range of wood stains commonly used on woodwork, it's not necessary to duplicate both the grain and the color of any particular wood. For wood graining glaze, mix two parts craft acrylic paint or latex paint and one part acrylic paint thickener.

Tools & Materials:

Synthetic-bristle paintbrush, sponge applicator or paint roller; wood-graining rocker; 3"- or 4"-wide soft natural-bristle paintbrush; pencil; straightedge; painter's masking tape; putty knife; low-luster latex enamel paint; craft acrylic paint or latex paint; acrylic paint thickener; rags; cardboard; satin or high-gloss clear finish or aerosol clear acrylic sealer.

How to Paint a Faux Wood Grain Finish

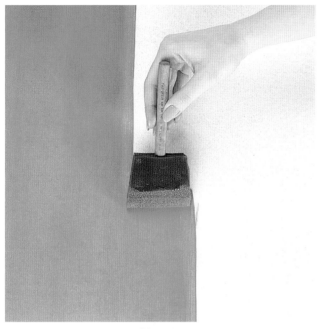

1 Apply a base coat of low-luster latex enamel in the desired color, stroking in the desired direction for the wood grain. Use a paintbrush or sponge applicator, or use a paint roller for large areas. Allow the paint to dry.

2 Mix the wood-graining glaze. Apply an even coat of glaze over the base coat, working in a small area at a time, using a sponge applicator or a synthetic-bristle paintbrush. Stroke the brush in the desired direction for the wood grain.

3 Slide the wood-graining rocker through the wet glaze, rocking it slowly to create the wood-grain effect. Starting at a corner, work in one continuous motion as you slide and rock the tool from one end to another. The position of the rocker corresponds to the wood grain markings, as shown here.

4 Repeat step 3 for subsequent rows, varying the space between oval markings. Wipe excess glaze from the tool as necessary, using a dry rag. For some rows, pull the comb or notched edge of the wood-graining tool through the glaze instead of using the rocker portion. This varies the look by giving it a simple, continuous wood grain.

5 Brush across the surface before the glaze is completely dry, using a dry, soft natural-bristle paintbrush, 3" to 4" wide. Lightly brush in the direction of the wood grain to soften the finish. Wipe excess glaze from the brush as necessary. Allow the glaze to dry. Apply a clear finish or aerosol clear acrylic sealer, if desired.

How to Paint a Faux Wood Parquet Finish

1 Apply a base coat of low-luster latex enamel, using a paintbrush or paint roller. Allow the paint to dry. Measure and mark a grid over the base coat, using a straightedge and pencil. Center the grid or begin with a complete square at one corner.

2 Apply painter's masking tape to alternate squares in the grid. Use a putty knife to trim the masking tape diagonally at the corners. Press firmly along the edges of tape to prevent the glaze from seeping through. Mix the wood-graining glaze.

3 Apply the glaze to the unmasked squares, brushing in a vertical direction. Slide the wood-graining rocker vertically through the wet glaze on some squares for a straight wood-grain effect. Rock the tool vertically on the remaining squares, varying the positions of the oval markings. Work on only a few squares at a time because the glaze dries quickly.

4 Brush across the surface before the glaze is completely dry, using a dry, soft, natural-bristle paintbrush. Brush lightly in the direction of the wood grain to soften the finish. Wipe excess glaze from the brush as necessary, using a dry rag.

5 Allow the glaze to dry, then remove the masking tape. Apply new tape over the wood-grained squares. Apply glaze to the unmasked squares, brushing in a horizontal direction. Repeat steps 3 and 4, working in a horizontal direction. Allow the paint to dry, then remove the tape. Apply a clear finish or aerosol clear acrylic sealer, if desired.

Wood Color Variations

Cherry wood is duplicated by using a dark, rust base coat and a burnt umber glaze.

Honey oak is mimicked by using a light tan base coat and a golden tan glaze.

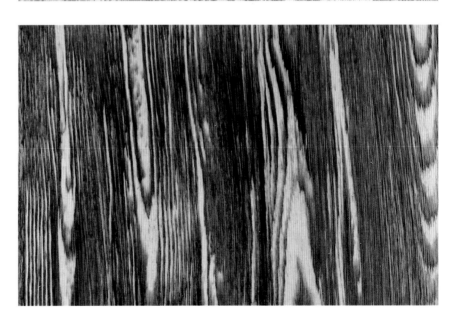

Walnut is imitated by using a dark gold base coat and a burnt umber glaze.

Painting Decorative Borders

A painted striped border with a block print design is a great way to add a personal touch to your floor. The stripes and designs effectively frame an attractive wood floor. The actual painting is the easy part of the project. The more time-consuming aspect is laying out the design on the floor and taping the paint lines. Take your time applying the tape to make sure it's pressed firmly to the floor, or paint could run under it.

Closed-cell foam for the block-print design is available as thin, pressure-sensitive sheets, neoprene weather-stripping tape, neoprene sheets, and computer mouse pads.

Tools & Materials:

Fine grit sandpaper, painter's masking tape, putty knife, straightedge, tape measure, vacuum, tack cloth, paintbrush, paint, closed-cell foam, wood block, acrylic paint extender, felt, glass or acrylic sheet, high-gloss clear finish, sponge applicator, satin clear finish.

How to Paint Decorative Borders

1 Sand the surface of a previously stained and sealed wood floor lightly in the area to be painted, using fine sandpaper, to degloss the finish and improve paint adhesion. Vacuum the entire floor, and wipe with tack cloth.

2 Measure and mark the design lines for the border on the floor, using a straightedge and pencil. Mask off stripes in the design, using painter's masking tape. Press the tape firmly along edges with a putty knife to prevent paint from seeping under the tape.

3 Apply paint for the stripes, using a paintbrush. Remove the masking tape. Allow the paint to dry.

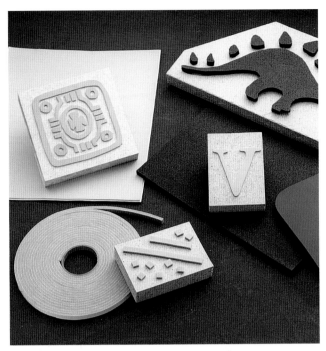

4 Make printing blocks from closed-cell foam that's cut to desired shapes and attached to a wood block.

5 Thin the paint slightly with an acrylic paint extender, about three to four parts paint to one part extender. Cut a piece of felt, larger than the printing block. Place the felt pad on glass or acrylic sheet. Pour the paint mixture onto the felt, allowing the paint to saturate the pad.

6 Press the printing block onto the felt pad, coating the surface of the foam evenly with paint.

7 Press the printing block onto the floor, applying firm, even pressure to the back of the block. Remove the block by pulling it straight back off the floor to avoid smudging. Apply a coat of high-gloss clear finish over the entire floor, using a sponge applicator. Allow the finish to dry, then sand lightly with fine-grit sandpaper. Wipe with tack cloth. Apply two coats of satin clear finish.

Creating Nature Print Floor Designs

Use leaves to create a unique imprint on your floor. Leaves can be collected from your own backyard or found at a local florist. Experiment with the printing process on paper to determine which leaves provide the desired finished result. Printing with the back side of the leaf may provide more detail in the finished print.

Nature print designs can be applied easily over previously stained or color-washed and finished floors. A wood floor can be embellished with

corner designs or a border. For a parquet floor, apply leaf prints randomly to the centers of the wood squares.

Tools & Materials:

Fine-grit sandpaper, tack cloth, synthetic brush, sponge applicator, wax paper, rubber brayer (about 4" wide), lint-free cloth, craft acrylic paints, high-gloss and satin clear finishes, fresh leaves.

How to Print Floor Designs

1 Press the leaves flat by placing them between pages of a large book for about an hour. Sand the surface of a previously stained and sealed wood floor lightly in the area to be printed, using fine-grit sandpaper. Wipe with a tack cloth. Apply a thin layer of craft acrylic paint to the back side of the leaf, using a sponge applicator.

2 Position the leaf, paint-side down, over the floor in the desired location of the print, then cover it with wax paper. Roll the brayer over the leaf to make an imprint. Carefully remove the wax paper and leaf. Remove any unwanted paint lines from the imprint, using a damp cloth before the paint dries. Allow the paint to dry. Repeat the printing process for a desired number of leaf prints. Apply two coats of clear finish over the designs.

Floors & Stair Repairs

Floor coverings wear out faster than other interior surfaces because they get more wear and tear. Surface damage can affect more than just appearance. Scratches in resilient flooring and cracks in grouted tile joints can let moisture into the floor's underpinnings. Hardwood floors lose their finish and become discolored. Loose boards squeak.

Underneath the finish flooring, moisture ruins wood underlayment and the damage is passed on to the subfloor. Bathroom floors suffer the most from moisture problems. Subflooring can pull loose from joists, causing floors to become uneven and springy.

Joist problems are less common, but their effects won't go unnoticed for long. A cracked or otherwise weakened joist may sag, causing a low spot in the floor and placing additional stress on neighboring joists, while a bulging joist will push a subfloor upward, pulling the fasteners loose and projecting a hump in the flooring surface.

A defective joist can be repaired, but problems that indicate serious structural failure require the attention of a professional. These include widespread sagging, an overstressed main beam, sunken support posts, and visible deterioration of foundation walls.

You can fix other problems yourself, such as squeaks, a broken stair tread, damaged baseboard and trim, and minor damage to floor coverings, with the tools and techniques shown on the following pages.

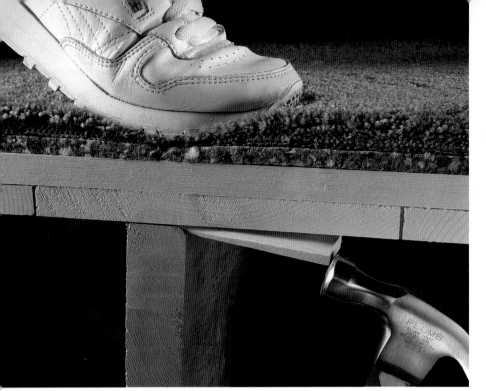

Eliminating Floor Squeaks

Floors squeak when floor-boards rub against each other or against the nails securing them to the subfloor. Hardwood floors squeak if they haven't been nailed properly. Normal changes in wood make some squeaking inevitable, although noisy floors sometimes indicate serious structural problems. If an area of a floor is soft or excessively squeaky, inspect the framing and the foundation supporting the floor.

Whenever possible, fix squeaks from underneath the floor. Joists longer than 8 feet should have X-bridging or solid blocking between each pair to help distribute the weight. If these supports aren't present, install them every 6 feet to stiffen and help silence a noisy floor.

Tools & Materials:

Drill, hammer, nail set, putty knife, wood screws, flooring nails, wood putty, graphite powder, dance-floor wax, pipe straps, hardwood shims, wood glue.

How to Eliminate Floor Squeaks

If you can access floor joists from underneath, drive wood screws up through the subfloor to draw hardwood flooring and the subfloor together. Drill pilot holes and make certain the screws aren't long enough to break through the top of the floorboards. Determine the combined thickness of the floor and subfloor by measuring at cutouts for pipes.

When you can't reach the floor from underneath, surface-nail the floor boards to the subfloor with ring-shank flooring nails. Drill pilot holes close to the tongue-side edge of the board and drive the nails at a slight angle to increase their holding power. Whenever possible, nail into studs. Countersink the nails with a nail set and fill the holes with tinted wood putty.

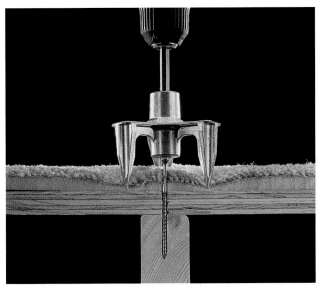

Eliminate squeaks in a carpeted floor by using a special floor fastening device, called a Squeeeeek No More, to drive screws through the subfloor into the joists. The device guides the screw and controls the depth. The screw has a scored shank, so once it's set, you can break the end off just below the surface of the subfloor.

Eliminate squeaks in hardwood floors with graphite powder, talcum powder, powdered soap, mineral oil, or liquid wax. Remove dirt and deposits from joints, using a putty knife. Apply graphite powder, talcum powder, powdered soap, or mineral oil between squeaky boards. Bounce on the boards to work the lubricant into the joints. Clean up excess powder with a damp cloth. Liquid wax is another option, although some floor finishes, such as urethane and varnish, are not compatible with wax, so check with the flooring manufacturer. Use a clean cloth to spread wax over the noisy joints, forcing the wax deep into the joints.

In an unfinished basement or crawl space, copper water pipes are usually hung from floor joists. Listen for pipes rubbing against joists. Loosen or replace wire pipe hangers to silence the noise. Pull the pointed ends of the hanger from the wood, using a hammer or pry bar. Lower the hanger just enough so the pipe isn't touching the joist, making sure the pipe is held firmly so it won't vibrate. Renail the hanger, driving the pointed end straight into the wood.

The boards or sheeting of a subfloor can separate from the joists, creating gaps. Where gaps are severe or appear above several neighboring joists, the framing may need reinforcement, but isolated gapping can usually be remedied with hardwood shims. Apply a small amount of wood glue to the shim and squirt some glue into the gap. Using a hammer, tap the shim into place until it's snug. Shimming too much will widen the gap, so be careful. Allow the glue to dry before walking on the floor.

Tread

Risers

Center stringer

Outside stringer

This staircase has center stringers to help support the treads. The 2 × 4s nailed between the outside stringers and the wall studs serve as spacers that allow room for the installation of skirt boards and wall finishes.

Eliminating Squeaks In Stairs

Like floors, stairs squeak when the lumber becomes warped or loose boards rub together. The continual pounding of foot traffic takes its toll on even the best built staircases. An unstable staircase is as unsafe as it is unattractive. Problems related to the structure of a staircase, such as severe sagging, twisting, or slanting, should be left to a professional. However, you can easily complete many common repairs.

Squeaks are usually caused by movement between the treads and risers, which can be alleviated from above or below the staircase.

If possible, fix squeaking stairs from underneath the staircase where you won't have to hide the repairs.

Tools & Materials:

Drill, screwdriver, hammer, utility knife, nail set, wood screws, wood putty, caulk gun, hardwood shims, wood plugs, wood glue, quarter-round molding, finish nails, construction adhesive.

How to Eliminate Squeaks from Below the Stairs

1 Glue wood blocks to the joints between the treads and risers with construction adhesive. Once the blocks are in place, drill pilot holes and fasten them to the treads and risers with wood screws. If the risers overlap the back edges of the treads, drive screws through the risers and into the treads to bind them together.

2 Fill the gaps between stair parts with tapered hardwood shims. Coat the shims with wood glue and tap them into the joints between treads and risers until they're snug. Shimming too much will widen the gap. Allow the glue to dry before walking on the stairs.

How to Eliminate Squeaks from Above the Stairs

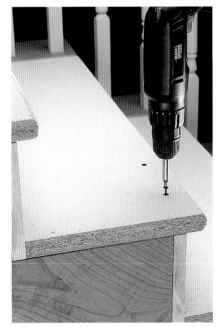

1 When the underside of a stair-case is inaccessible, silence noisy stairs from above. Drill pilot holes and drive screws down through stair treads into the risers. Countersink the screws and fill the holes with putty or wood plugs.

2 Tap glued wood shims under loose treads to keep them from flexing. Use a block to prevent splitting, and drive the shim just until it's snug. When the glue dries, cut the shims flush, using a utility knife.

3 Support the joints between treads and risers by attaching quarter-round molding. Drill pilot holes and use finish nails to fasten the molding. Set the nails with a nail set.

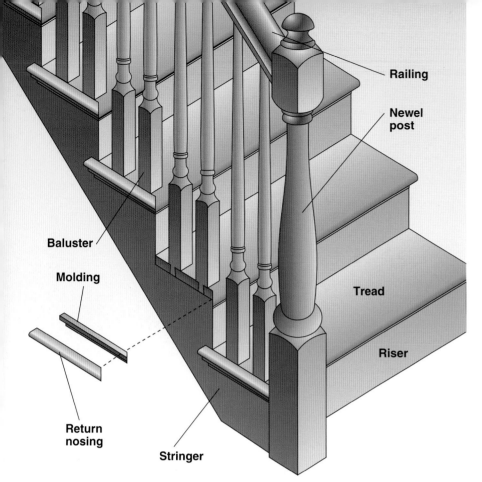

Railing

Newel post

Baluster

Molding

Tread

Return nosing

Stringer

Riser

Replacing a Broken Stair Tread

A broken stair tread is hazardous because we often don't look at steps as we climb them. Replace a broken step right away. The difficulty of this job depends on the construction of your staircase and the accessibility of the underside. It's better to replace a damaged tread than to repair it. A patch could create an irregular step that surprises someone unfamiliar with it.

Tools & Materials:

Flat pry bar, hammer, combination square, circular saw, drill, nail set, caulk gun, stair tread, construction adhesive, screws, wood putty, finish nails, nail set.

How to Replace a Broken Stair Tread

1 Carefully remove any decorative elements attached to the tread. Pull up carpeting and roll it aside. Remove trim pieces on or around the edges of the tread. Remove the balusters by detaching the top ends from the railing and separating the joints in the tread. Some staircases have a decorative hardwood cap inlaid into each tread. Remove these with a flat pry bar, taking care to pry from underneath the cap to avoid marring the exposed edges.

2 If possible, hammer upward from underneath the stairs to separate the tread from the risers and stringers. Otherwise, use a hammer and pry bar to work the tread loose, pulling nails as you go. Once the tread is removed, scrape the exposed edges of the stringers to remove old glue and wood fragments.

3 Measure the length for the new tread and mark it with a combination square so the cut end will be square and straight. If the tread has a milled end for an inlay, cut from the plain end. Cut the new tread to size, using a circular saw, and test-fit it carefully.

4 Apply a bead of construction adhesive to the exposed tops of the stringers. The adhesive will strengthen the bond between the tread and stringer and will cushion the joint, preventing the parts from squeaking.

5 Set the tread in place. If you have access to the step from underneath, secure the tread to the riser above it by driving screws through the riser into the back edge of the tread. To fasten it from the top side, drill and countersink pilot holes and drive two or three screws through the tread into the top edge of each stringer. Also drive a few screws along the front edge of the tread into the riser below it. Fill the screw holes in the tread with wood putty or plugs.

6 Reinstall any decorative elements, using finish nails. Set the nails with a nail set. Reinstall the balusters, if necessary.

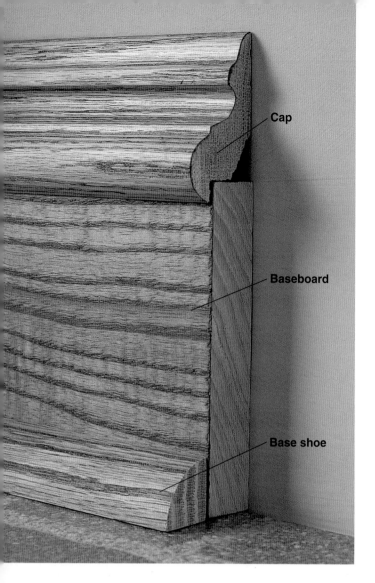

Cap

Baseboard

Base shoe

Removing & Replacing Trim Moldings

There's no reason to let damaged trim moldings detract from the appearance of a well-maintained room. With the right tools and a little attention to detail, you can replace or repair them quickly and easily.

Home centers and lumber yards sell many styles of moldings, but they may not stock moldings found in older homes. If you have trouble finding duplicates, check salvage yards in your area. They sometimes carry styles no longer manufactured. You can also try combining several different moldings to duplicate a more elaborate version.

Tools & Materials:

Flat pry bars (2); coping saw; miter saw; drill; hammer; nail set; wood scraps; replacement moldings; 2d, 4d, and 6d finish nails; wood putty.

How to Remove Damaged Trim

1 To remove baseboards without damaging the wall, use leverage rather than force. Pry off the base shoe first, using a flat pry bar. When you feel a few nails pop, move farther along the molding and pry again.

2 Even the lightest pressure from a pry bar can damage wallboard or plaster, so use a large, flat scrap of wood to protect the wall. Insert one bar beneath the trim and work the other bar between the baseboard and the wall. Force the pry bars in opposite directions to remove the baseboard.

How to Install Baseboards

1 Start at an inside corner by butting one piece of baseboard securely into the corner. Drill pilot holes, then fasten the baseboard with two 6d finish nails, aligned vertically, at each wall stud. Cut a scrap of baseboard so the ends are perfectly square. Cut the end of the workpiece square. Position the scrap on the back of the workpiece so its back face is flush with the end of the workpiece. Trace the outline of the scrap onto the back of the workpiece.

2 Cut along the outline on the workpiece with a coping saw, keeping the saw perpendicular to the baseboard face. Test-fit the coped end. Recut it, if necessary.

3 To cut the baseboard to fit at outside corners, mark the end where it meets the outside wall corner. Cut the end at a 45° angle, using a power miter saw. Lock-nail all miter joints by drilling a pilot hole and driving 4d finish nails through each corner.

4 Install base shoe molding along the bottom of the baseboards. Make miter joints at inside and outside corners, and fasten base shoe with 2d finish nails. Whenever possible, complete a run of molding using one piece. For long spans, join molding pieces by mitering the ends at parallel 45° angles. Set nail heads below the surface using a nail set, then fill the holes with wood putty.

Replacing Damaged Floor Boards

When solid hardwood floorboards are beyond repair, they need to be carefully cut out and replaced with boards of the same width and thickness. Replace whole boards whenever possible. If a board is long, or if part of its length is inaccessible, draw a cutting line across the face of the board, and tape behind the line to protect the section that will remain.

Tools & Materials:

Drill, spade bit, circular saw, chisel, hammer, caulk gun, nail set, replacement boards, masking tape, construction adhesive, spiral-shank flooring nails, nail set, wood putty.

How to Replace Damaged Floor Boards

1 Draw a cutting line across the face of the damaged board and tape behind the line. Drill several overlapping holes at the ends of the board or just inside the cutting lines, using a spade bit. Set the depth of your circular saw to the exact thickness of the floor boards, then make several cuts through the middle of each board. Cut outward from the center until the saw cuts intersect the holes.

2 Chisel out the center of the board, working out to the edges. Don't pry or drive the chisel against any good boards.

3 To complete a cut in the middle of a board, square off the edge at the cutting line, using a sharp, wide chisel.

4 Cut the replacement boards to fit and install them one at a time. Apply construction adhesive to the bottom face and in the groove of the board, and set it in place. Drill pilot holes and drive spiral-shank flooring nails at a 45° angle through the base of the tongue and into the subfloor. Set the nails with a nail set.

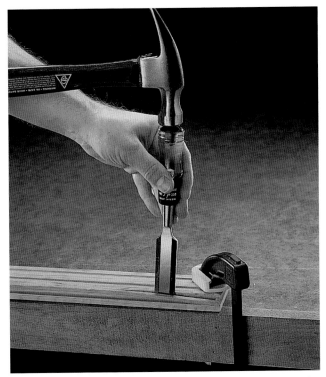

5 To install the last board, chisel off the lower lip of the groove. Remove the tongue on the end of the board, if necessary. Apply adhesive to the board, and set it in place, tongue first.

6 Drive flooring nails through the top of the board at both ends and along the groove side. Set the nails with a nail set and fill the nail holes with wood putty.

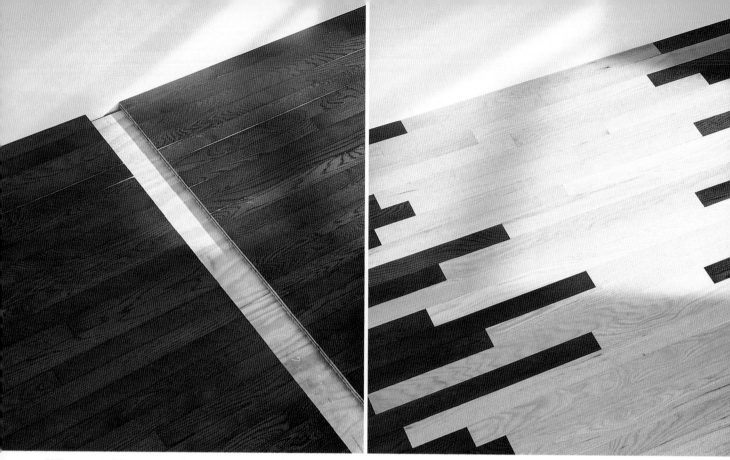

When patching a wood-strip floor, one option is to remove all of the floor boards that butt against the flooring gap using a pry bar and replace them with boards cut to fit. This may require you to trim the tongues from some tongue-andgroove floorboards. Sand and refinish the entire floor so the new boards match the old.

Patching Flooring

When an interior wall or section of wall has been removed during remodeling, you'll need to patch gaps in the flooring where the wall was located. There are several options for patching floors, depending on your budget and the level of your do-it-yourself skills.

If the existing flooring shows signs of wear, consider replacing the entire flooring surface. Although it can be expensive, an entirely new floor covering will completely hide any gaps in the floor and provide an elegant finishing touch for your remodeling project.

If you choose to patch the existing flooring, be aware that it's difficult to hide patched areas completely, especially if the flooring uses unique patterns or finishes. A creative solution is to intentionally patch the floor with material that contrasts with the surrounding flooring (opposite page).

A quick, inexpensive solution is to install T-molding to bridge a gap in a wood strip floor. T-moldings are especially useful when the surrounding boards run parallel to the gap. T-moldings are available in several widths and can be stained to match the flooring.

How to Use Contrasting Flooring Material

Fill gaps in floors with materials that have a contrasting color and pattern. For wood floors, parquet tiles are an easy and inexpensive choice (above, left). You may need to widen the gap with a circular saw set to the depth of the wood covering to make room for the contrasting tiles. To enhance the effect, cut away a border strip around the room and fill these areas with the same contrasting flooring material (above, right).

Tips for Patching Floors

Build up the subfloor in the patch area, using layers of thin plywood and building paper, so the new surface will be flush with the surrounding flooring. You may need to experiment with different combinations of plywood and paper to find the right thickness.

Make a vinyl or carpet patch by laying the patch material over the old flooring, then cutting through both layers. When the cut strip of old flooring is removed, the new patch will fit tightly in its place. If flooring material is patterned, make sure the patterns are aligned before you cut.

Install a carpet patch using heat-activated carpet tape and a rented seam iron. Original carpet remnants are ideal for patching. New carpet, even of the same brand, style and color, will seldom match the original carpet exactly.

Repairing Vinyl Floor Coverings

Repair methods for vinyl flooring depend on the type of floor as well as the type of damage. With sheet vinyl, you can fuse the surface or patch in new material. With vinyl tile, it's best to replace the damaged tiles.

Small cuts and scratches can be fused permanently and nearly invisibly with liquid seam sealer, a clear compound that's available wherever vinyl flooring is sold. For tears or burns, the damaged area can be patched. If necessary, remove vinyl from a hidden area, such an the inside of a closet or under an appliance, to use as patch material.

When vinyl flooring is badly worn or the damage is widespread, the only answer is complete re-placement. Although it's possible to add layers of flooring in some situations, evaluate the options carefully. Be aware that the backing of older vinyl tiles made of asphalt may contain asbestos fibers. Consult a professional for their removal.

Tools & Materials:

Carpenter's square, utility knife, putty knife, heat gun, J-roller, notched trowel, marker, masking tape, scrap of matching flooring, mineral spirits, floor covering adhesive, wax paper, liquid seam sealer.

How to Repair Vinyl Floor Covering

1 Select a scrap patch of vinyl that matches the existing floor. Place the patch over the damaged area and adjust it until the pattern matches. Tape the patch to the floor.

2 Use a carpenter's square to outline the patch. Draw along pattern lines to conceal patch seams. Use a utility knife to cut through both layers of vinyl. Remove the damaged vinyl with a putty knife.

3 Apply mineral spirits to dissolve adhesive, then scrape the subfloor clean with a putty knife or razor scraper. Apply new adhesive to the patch, then fit the patch in the hole. Roll the patch with a J-roller, then let it dry for 24 hours. Apply a thin bead of liquid seam sealer to the patch edges.

How to Replace Vinyl Floor Tiles

1 Use a heat gun to soften the underlying adhesive. Move the gun rapidly, being careful not to melt the tile. When the adhesive gives way, lift the tile out with a putty knife.

2 Apply mineral spirits to dissolve any remaining adhesive. Scrape away all residue, using a putty knife. If necessary, repair the underlayment.

3 Apply new adhesive to the underlayment with a notched trowel. Position the new tile in the hole. Roll the tile using pressure to create a good bond. Wipe off any excess adhesive.

Repairing Carpeting

Burns and stains are the most common carpeting problems. You can clip away the burned fibers of superficial burns using small scissors. Deeper burns and indelible stains require patching by cutting away and replacing the damaged area.

Another common problem, addressed on the opposite page, is carpet seams or edges that have come loose. You can rent the tools necessary for fixing this problem.

Tools & Materials:

Cookie-cutter tool, knee kicker, 4" wallboard knife, utility knife, seam iron, replacement carpeting, double-face carpet tape, seam adhesive, heat-activated seam tape, boards, weights.

How to Repair Spot Damage

1 Remove extensive damage or stains with a "cookie-cutter" tool, available at carpeting stores. Press the cutter down over the damaged area and twist it to cut away the carpet.

2 Using the cookie cutter tool again, cut a replacement patch from scrap carpeting. Insert double-face carpet tape under the cutout, positioning the tape so it overlaps the patch seams.

3 Press the patch into place. Make sure the direction of the nap or pattern matches the existing carpet. To seal the seam and prevent unraveling, apply seam adhesive to the edges of the patch.

How to Restretch Loose Carpeting

1 Adjust the knob on the head of the knee kicker so the prongs grab the carpet backing without penetrating through the padding. Starting from a corner or near a point where the carpet is firmly attached, press the knee kicker head into the carpet, about 2" from the wall.

2 Thrust your knee into the cushion of the knee kicker to force the carpet toward the wall. Tuck the carpet edge into the space between the wood strip and the baseboard using a 4" wallboard knife. If the carpet is still loose, trim the edge with a utility knife and stretch it again.

How to Reglue Loose Seams

1 Remove the old tape from under the carpet seam. Cut a strip of new seam tape and place it under the carpet so it's centered along the seam with the adhesive facing up. Plug in the seam iron and let it heat up.

2 Pull up both edges of the carpet and set the hot iron squarely onto the tape. Wait about 30 seconds for the glue to melt. Move the iron about 12" farther along the seam. Quickly press the edges of the carpet together into the melted glue behind the iron. Separate the pile to make sure no fibers are stuck in the glue and the seam is tight. Place weighted boards over the seam to keep it flat while the glue sets. Remember, you have only 30 seconds to repeat the process.

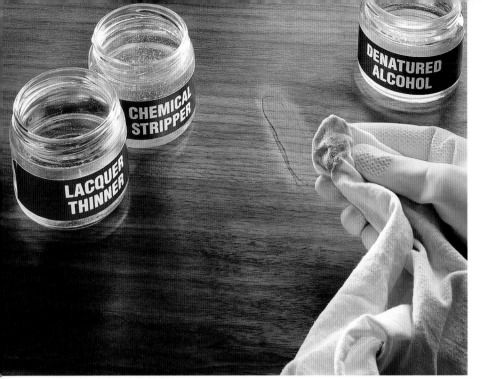

Identify surface finishes using solvents. In an inconspicuous area, rub in different solvents to see if the finish dissolves, softens, or is removed. Denatured alcohol removes shellac, while lacquer thinner removes lacquer. If neither of those work, try nail polish remover containing acetone, which removes varnish but not polyurethane.

Tools & Materials:

Vacuum, buffing machine, hammer, nail set, putty knife, cloths, hardwood cleaning kit, paste wax, rubber gloves, oxalic acid, vinegar, wood restorer, latex wood patch, sandpaper.

Repairing Hardwood Flooring

Often, a darkened, dingy hardwood floor needs only a thorough cleaning to reveal an attractive, healthy finish. If you have a fairly new or prefinished hardwood floor, check with the manufacturer or flooring installer before applying any cleaning products or wax. Most prefinished hardwood, for example, should not be waxed.

Water and other liquids can penetrate deep into the grain of hardwood floor boards, leaving dark stains that are sometimes impossible to remove by sanding. Instead, try bleaching the wood with oxalic acid, available in crystal form at home centers or paint stores.

When gouges, scratches, and dents aren't bad enough to warrant replacing a floorboard, repair the damaged area with a latex wood patch that matches the color of your floor.

How to Clean & Renew Hardwood

1 Vacuum the entire floor. Mix hot water and dishwashing detergent that doesn't contain lye, trisodium phosphate, or ammonia. Working on 3-ft.-square sections, scrub the floor with a brush or nylon scrubbing pad. Wipe up the water and wax with a towel before moving to the next section.

2 If the water and detergent don't remove the old wax, use a hardwood floor cleaning kit. Use only solvent-type cleaners, as some water-based products can blacken wood. Apply the cleaner following the manufacturer's instructions.

3 When the floor is clean and dry, apply a high-quality floor wax. Paste wax is more difficult to apply than liquid floor wax, but it lasts much longer. Apply the wax by hand, then polish the floor with a rented buffing machine fitted with synthetic buffing pads.

How to Remove Stains

  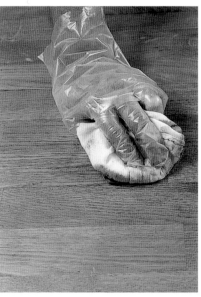

1 Remove the floor's finish by sanding the stained area with sandpaper. In a disposable cup, dissolve the recommended amount of oxalic acid crystals in water. Wearing rubber gloves, pour the mixture over the stained area, taking care to cover only the darkened wood.

2 Let the liquid stand for one hour. Repeat the application, if necessary. Wash with 2 tablespoons borax dissolved in one pint water to neutralize the acid. Rinse with water, and let the wood dry. Sand the area smooth.

3 Apply several coats of wood restorer until the bleached area matches the finish of the surrounding floor.

How to Patch Scratches & Small Holes

1 Before filling nail holes, make sure the nails are securely set in the wood. Use a hammer and nail set to drive loose nails below the surface. Apply wood patch to the damaged area, using a putty knife. Force the compound into the hole by pressing the knife blade downward until it lies flat on the floor.

2 Scrape excess compound from the edges, and allow the patch to dry completely. Sand the patch flush with the surrounding surface. Using fine-grit sandpaper, sand in the direction of the wood grain.

3 Apply wood restorer to the sanded area until it blends with the rest of the floor.

Apply grout sealer to joints every 1 to 2 years to protect against water, wear, and stains. Use a sponge brush to spread the sealer and keep it off the tiles. Allow new grout to cure before sealing it.

Repairing Ceramic Flooring

Although ceramic tile is one of the hardest floor coverings, the tiles do sometimes become damaged and need to be replaced. Major cracks in grout joints indicate that movement of the floor has caused the adhesive layer beneath the tile to deteriorate. The adhesive layer must be replaced in order to create a permanent repair.

Any time you remove tile, check the underlayment. If it's no longer smooth, solid, and level, repair or replace it before replacing the tile.

When removing grout or damaged tiles, be careful not to damage surrounding tiles. Always

wear eye protection when working with a hammer and chisel.

Tools & Materials:

Hammer, cold chisel, eye protection, putty knife, square-notched trowel, rubber mallet, level, needlenose pliers, screwdriver, grout float mix, thin-set mortar, replacement tile, tile spacers, grout, bucket, grout pigment, grout sealer, grout sponge, floor-leveling compound.

How to Replace Ceramic Tile Floor

1 Remove the grout using a hammer and cold chisel. Hold the chisel at a slight angle and break away small sections of grout at a time. Clean the joints with a stiff-bristled broom or vacuum. When the joints are clean, use the hammer and cold chisel to break away the damaged tile. Drive the chisel down into a crack near the center of the tile, angling the piece forward and away. Work outward from the center until the tile is removed.

2 In rooms where the floor is often exposed to water, the underlayment should be cementboard. In other types of rooms, the underlayment may be plywood. In either case, scrape away any adhesive or mortar, leaving the underlayment smooth and flat. If necessary, fill chips or dents in the underlayment, using an epoxy-based thin-set mortar for cementboard or a floor-leveling compound for plywood.

3 Apply thin-set mortar to the back of the replacement tile, using a notched trowel to furrow the mortar. If replacing several tiles, use plastic spacers to ensure consistent spacing. Set the tile in position and press down on it until it's even with adjacent tiles.

4 Using a rubber mallet, gently rap the central area of the tile a few times to set it evenly into the mortar. Check the area with a level. If necessary to bring the tile level, lay a flat piece of 2 × 4 padded with carpet across several tiles, and rap it with the mallet.

5 Remove any spacers with needlenose pliers. Clean wet mortar from the grout joints with a small screwdriver, and wipe the mortar from the tile surfaces. Let the mortar dry for 24 hours. Fill the joints with grout that matches the existing grout color. Apply grout sealer with a small paintbrush.

Glossary

Adhesive — Bonding agent used to adhere the floor covering to the underlayment. Adhesives are also available for installing a floor covering on nonporous surfaces, such as sheet vinyl.

Air bubbles — Pockets of air that get trapped under resilient sheet flooring, an indication that the adhesive has failed.

American National Standards Institute (ANSI) — A standards-making organization that rates tile for water permeability.

Baseboard — Strip of wood molding, available in various designs and thicknesses, applied at the bottom of the wall to cover the gap between the floor covering and the wall.

Baseboard shoe — A narrow piece of molding, often quarter round, attached to the bottom of baseboard to hide gaps between the floor covering and baseboard, and to add a decorative edge.

Baseboard tile — Baseboard-shaped tile used instead of wood baseboards. Used in conjunction with tile floors.

Batter boards — Temporary stake structures used for positioning layout strings for outdoor floors.

Beam — Any horizontal framing member such as a joist or header.

Berber carpet — Looped pile running in parallel lines. Berber carpet has the same color throughout the fibers.

Blindnail — Driving nails at an angle through the tongues of hardwood flooring so the next piece of flooring will cover the nail.

Border — Wood or tile of a different color or style than the main floor covering that's installed along the edge of a floor or around a design to add a decorative element.

Building code — A set of building regulations and ordinances regulating the way a house can be built or remodeled. Most building codes are controlled by a local municipality.

Building permit — Permit obtained from the local building department allowing you to remodel your home.

Carpet bar — A metal bar providing a transition between carpet and another floor covering that's at the same height or lower than the bottom of carpet.

Cementboard — Underlayment used for ceramic tile and some hardwood installations. Cementboard is the best underlayment in areas likely to get wet.

Chalk line — The line left by chalk, usually blue or red, after the chalk string is pulled tight between two points and snapped against the floor.

Clear finish — A wood finish that allows the wood grain to be seen without discoloring the wood.

Coefficient of friction — The measure of a tile's slip resistance. Tiles with high numbers are more slip resistant.

Common nail — A heavy-shaft nail used primarily for framing work, available from 2d to 60d.

Cross bridging — Diagonal braces installed between joists to keep them from moving and to keep floors from squeaking. Cross bridging can be wood or metal.

Crosscut — Cutting a piece of wood perpendicular to the wood grain.

Cut-pile carpet — Individual carpet fibers woven tightly together. The fibers are colored on the outside, but not on the inside.

Door casing — Wood molding and trim placed around a door opening to give it a finished look.

Dry fit — Installing tile without mortar to test the layout.

Dry mix — Packaged mix, usually sold in bags, that can be combined with water to form mortar.

Embossing leveler — A mortar-like substance used to prepare resilient flooring or ceramic tile for use as an underlayment.

Endnail — Driving nails through the face of one board into the end of another one.

Engineered flooring — Flooring that's manufactured to look like solid hardwood, but is easier to install, less expensive, and more resistant to wear. Engineered flooring is available in strips or planks.

Expansion joint — A joint in a tile layout filled with a flexible material, such as caulk, instead of grout. The expansion joint allows the tile to shift without cracking.

Facenail — Driving nails into the face of tongue-and-groove flooring.

Fiber/cementboard underlayment — A thin, high-density underlayment used under ceramic tile and resilient flooring where floor height is a concern.

Field tile — Tile that's not part of a design or border.

Finish nail — A nail with a small, dimpled head, used for fastening wood trim and other detailed work.

Flagstone — Quarried stone cut into slabs usually less than 3" thick, used for outdoor floors.

Floating floor — Wood or laminate floor covering that rests on a thin foam padding and is not fastened or bonded to the subfloor or underlayment.

Floor board — A strip or plank in a wood floor.

Floor tile — Any type of tile designated for use on floors.

Floor-warming systems — A system of heating elements installed directly under the floor covering. Floor-warming systems provide supplemental radiant heat to warm up a floor.

Framing member — A common

term for a single structural element of a construction framework, such as a stud, joist, truss, or beam.

Full-spread vinyl — Sheet vinyl with a felt-paper backing that is secured to the underlayment with adhesive.

Grout — A dry powder, usually cement-based, that is mixed with water and pressed into the joints between tiles. Grout also comes with latex or acrylic additive for greater adhesion and impermeability.

Horizontal span — The horizontal distance a stairway covers.

Isolation membrane — A flexible material installed in sheets or troweled onto an unstable or damaged base floor or subfloor before installing tile. Isolation membrane prevents shifts in the base from damaging the tile above.

Jamb — The top and side pieces that make up the finished frame of a door opening.

Joists — The framing members that support the floor.

Latex patching compound — Compound used to fill cracks and chips in old underlayment and to cover screw or nail heads and seams in new underlayment.

Level — A line or plane that is parallel to the surface of still water.

Longstrip flooring — Wood flooring that has multiple strips, usually three, fastened together to form a single plank.

Medallion — Wood or tile design placed in a floor as a decoration.

Miter cut — An angle cut in the end of a piece of flooring or molding.

Molding — Decorative strips of wood installed along walls and floors.

Natural stone tile — Tile cut from marble, slate, granite, or other natural stone.

On center — The distance from the center of one framing member to the center of the next.

Perimeter-bond vinyl — Sheet vinyl with a PVC backing that is placed directly on underlayment and secured by adhesives along the edges and seams.

Planks — Wood or laminate flooring that is 4" or more wide.

Plywood — A common underlayment for resilient and ceramic tile installations.

Portland cement — A combination of silica, lime, iron, and alumina that has been heated, cooled, and pulverized to form a fine powder from which mortar products are made.

PVC — Acronym for polyvinyl chloride. PVC is a rigid plastic material that is highly resistant to heat and chemicals.

Reducers — Strips of wood that provide a transition from a hardwood floor to an adjacent floor of lower height.

Reference lines — Lines marked on the subfloor to guide the placement of the floor covering.

Rip — Cutting a piece of wood parallel to the grain.

Rise — The height of a step in a stairway.

Riser — A board attached to the front of a step between treads in a stairway.

Run — The length of a step in a stairway.

Sealants — Product used to protect non- and semi-vitreous tile from stains and water damage. Sealants are also used to protect grout.

Sheet vinyl — Flooring material made from vinyl and other plastics in the form of sheets that are 6 ft. or 12 ft. wide and approximately ⅛" thick.

Sistering — Fastening a new floor joist to a damaged floor joist for additional strength.

Sleepers — Boards placed over a concrete floor and used to support the subflooring of a new floor.

Spacers — Plastic lugs inserted between tiles to help maintain uniform installation during installation.

Stain — Water-based or oil-based agent used to penetrate and change the color of a wood floor.

Strips — Wood or laminate flooring that is less than 4" wide.

Subfloor — The surface, usually made of plywood, attached to the floor joists.

Tack cloth — Lint free cloth, usually cheese cloth, used to clean floors and wipe away dust. Tack cloth is treated with a resin to make it sticky.

Tackless strips — Strips of wood nailed around the perimeter of a room. The teeth of the strips hold carpet in place.

Threshold — The area in a doorway where two floor coverings meet.

Toenail — Driving a nail at a 45° through the side of one board into the face of another one.

Tongue-and-groove flooring — Wood or laminate floor coverings that have a tongue and a groove in each individual piece. The flooring is assembled by placing the tongue and groove joints together.

Underlayment — Material placed on top of the subfloor, such as plywood, fiber/cementboard, cementboard, and isolation membrane.

Vapor barrier — Plastic sheeting used as a barrier to keep water from a concrete floor from penetrating the floor covering installed over it.

Waterproofing membrane — A flexible, waterproof material installed in sheets or brushed on to protect the subfloor from water damage.

Contributors

Blackstock Leather, Inc.
13452 Kennedy Road
Stouffville, Ontario L4A 7X5, Canada
800-663-6657
Photo on p. 28 (top) by photographer
Hennie Reaymakers

Buddy Rhodes Studio
877-706-5303
www.buddyrhodes.com
Photo on p. 141 (right) by photographer,
Ken Gutmaker; Kitchen design,
www.johnnygrey.com

Crossville Porcelain Stone
P.O. Box 1168
Crossville, TN 38557
(931) 484-2110
www.crossvilleceramics.com

Daltile
7834 C.F. Hawn Freeway
Dallas, TX 75217
800-933-TILE
www.daltile.com

Edelman Leather
80 Pickett District Road
New Milford, CT 06776
800-886-TEDY
www.edelmanleather.com

Expanko Cork Company, Inc.
3027 Lower Valley Road
Parkesburg, PA 19365
800-345-6202
www.expanko.com

Floors of Distinction
12642 Bass Lake Road
Maple Grove, MN 55369
763-553-1800

IKEA Home Furnishings
496 W. Germantown Pike
Plymouth Meeting, PA 19462
800-434-4532
www.ikea-usa.com

Kaswell & Company
58 Pearl Street
Framingham, MA 01701
508-879-1120
www.kaswell.com

Kentucky Wood Floors
PO Box 33276
Louisville, KY 40232
502-451-6024
www.kentuckywood.com

Marmoleum by Forbo Linoleum
Humboldt Ind. Park
PO Box 667
Hazelton, PA 18201
800-842-7839
www.themarmoleumstore.com

Mirage/Boa-Franc Inc.
1255 98 Rue
St. Goerges, Quebec, G5Y 8J5 Canada
800-463-1303
www.boa-franc.com

Mohawk Industries
235 S. Industrial Boulevard
Calhoun, GA 30701
800-2MOHAWK
www.mohawk-flooring.com

My-Grain Creative Woodwork
216 W. Roberts Street
P.O. Box 161
Holmen, WI 54636
800-481-5476
www.my-grain.com

Natural Cork Flooring
1710 North Leg Court
Augusta, GA 30909
800-404-2675
www.naturalcork.com

Ceramic Tiles of Italy
212-980-1500

To find local dealers for Ceramic Tiles
of Italy visit www.italytile.com

p. 145 Ariana www.ariana.it

p. 165 (bottom left) Castlevetro
www.castlevetro.it

p. 21 Girardi www.girardi.it

p. 165 (bottom right) Nordica
www.nordica.it

Oshkosh Floor Designs
911 E. Main Street
Winneconne, WI 54986
920-582-9977
www.oshkoshfloors.com

Patina Old World Flooring
3820 North Ventura Avenue
Ventura, CA 93001
800-501-1113
www.patinawoodfloors.com

Pergo, Inc.
3128 Highwoods Boulevard
Raleigh, NC 27604
800-33-PERGO
www.pergo.com

Robus Leather Corporation
1100 West Hutchinson Lane
Madison, IN 47250
812-273-4183
www.blackpearltiles.com
www.robus.com

TimberGrass Fine Bamboo Flooring
12715 Miller Road NE
Bainbridge Island, WA 98110
800-929-6333
www.timbergrass.com

Timeless Timber Inc.
2200 E. Lake Shore Drive
Ashland, WI 54806
888-653-5647
www.timelesstimber.com

Walker & Zanger, Inc.
13190 Telfair Avenue
Sylmar, CA 91342
818-504-0235
www.walkerzanger.com

Wilsonart International
33 Center Street
Temple, TX 76503
800-710-8846
www.wilsonart.com

Photographers

Beateworks, Inc.
Los Angeles, CA
www.beateworks.com

©Henry Cabala/Beateworks.com: p. 173

©Christopher Covey/Beateworks.com:
p. 141 (left)

©Douglas Hill/Beateworks.com: p. 23
(top)

©Inside/Beateworks.com: pp. 17
(top), 20 (bottom), 21 (bottom), 23
(bottom), 26 (bottom), 33, 88 (top),
101, 125 (right), 165 (top right)

©Tim Street-Porter/Beateworks.com:
p. 22 (bottom)

Corbis
www.corbis.com
©Elizabeth Whiting & Associates/
Corbis: p. 102 (bottom)

Getty Images
www.gettyimages.com

©Getty Images/Janis Christie: p. 27
(bottom)

©Getty Images/Ryan McVay: p. 27 (top)

Additional Resources

American Society of Interior Designers
202-546-3480
www.asid.org

Association of Home Appliance Manufacturers
202-872-5955
www.aham.org

Carpet and Rug Institute
800-882-8846
www.carpet-rug.com

Center for Universal Design NC State University
919-515-3082
www.design.ncsu.edu/cud

Construction Materials Recycling Association
630-548-4510
www.cdrecycling.org

Energy & Environmental Building Association
952-881-1098
www.eeba.org

International Residential Code Book International Conference of Building Officials
800-284-4406
www.icbo.com

Maple Flooring Manufacturers Association
847-480-9138
www.maplefloor.org

National Kitchen & Bath Association (NKBA)
800-843-6522
www.nkba.org

National Wood Flooring Association
800-422-4556
www.woodfloors.org

Resilient Floor Covering Institute
301-340-8580
www.rfci.com

The Tile Council of America, Inc.
864-646-8453
www.tileusa.com

U.S. Environmental Protection Agency—Indoor Air Quality
www.epa.gov/iedweb00/pubs/insidest.html

Wood Floor Covering Association
800-624-6880
www.wfca.org

Wood Flooring Manufacturers Association
901-526-5016
www.nofma.org

Conversion Charts

Lumber Dimensions

Nominal - U.S.	Actual - U.S.	Metric	Nominal - U.S.	Actual - U.S.	Metric
1 × 2	¾" × 1½"	19 × 38 mm	1½ × 4	1¼" × 3½"	32 × 89 mm
1 × 3	¾" × 2½"	19 × 64 mm	1½ × 6	1¼" × 5½"	32 × 140 mm
1 × 4	¾" × 3½"	19 × 89 mm	1½ × 8	1¼" × 7¼"	32 × 184 mm
1 × 5	¾" × 4½"	19 × 114 mm	1½ × 10	1¼" × 9¼"	32 × 235 mm
1 × 6	¾" × 5½"	19 × 140 mm	1½ × 12	1¼" × 11¼"	32 × 286 mm
1 × 7	¾" × 6¼"	19 × 159 mm	2 × 4	1½" × 3½"	38 × 89 mm
1 × 8	¾" × 7¼"	19 × 184 mm	2 × 6	1½" × 5½"	38 × 140 mm
1 × 10	¾" × 9¼"	19 × 235 mm	2 × 8	1½" × 7¼"	38 × 184 mm
1 × 12	¾" × 11¼"	19 × 286 mm	2 × 10	1½" × 9¼"	38 × 235 mm
1¼ × 4	1" × 3½"	25 × 89 mm	2 × 12	1½" × 11¼"	38 × 286 mm
1¼ × 6	1" × 5½"	25 × 140 mm	3 × 6	2½" × 5½"	64 × 140 mm
1¼ × 8	1" × 7¼"	25 × 184 mm	4 × 4	3½" × 3½"	89 × 89 mm
1¼ × 10	1" × 9¼"	25 × 235 mm	4 × 6	3½" × 5½"	89 × 140 mm
1¼ × 12	1" × 11¼"	25 × 286 mm			

Metric Conversions

To Convert:	To:	Multiply by:	To Convert:	To:	Multiply by:
Inches	Millimeters	25.4	Millimeters	Inches	0.039
Inches	Centimeters	2.54	Centimeters	Inches	0.394
Feet	Meters	0.305	Meters	Feet	3.28
Yards	Meters	0.914	Meters	Yards	1.09
Square inches	Square centimeters	6.45	Square centimeters	Square inches	0.155
Square feet	Square meters	0.093	Square meters	Square feet	10.8
Square yards	Square meters	0.836	Square meters	Square yards	1.2
Ounces	Milliliters	30.0	Milliliters	Ounces	.033
Pints (U.S.)	Liters	0.473 (Imp. 0.568)	Liters	Pints (U.S.)	2.114 (Imp. 1.76)
Quarts (U.S.)	Liters	0.946 (Imp. 1.136)	Liters	Quarts (U.S.)	1.057 (Imp. 0.88)
Gallons (U.S.)	Liters	3.785 (Imp. 4.546)	Liters	Gallons (U.S.)	0.264 (Imp. 0.22)
Ounces	Grams	28.4	Grams	Ounces	0.035
Pounds	Kilograms	0.454	Kilograms	Pounds	2.2

Counterbore, Shank & Pilot Hole Diameters

Screw Size	Counterbore Diameter for Screw Head	Clearance Hole for Screw Shank	Pilot Hole Diameter	
			Hard Wood	Soft Wood
#1	.146 (9/64)	5/64	3/64	1/32
#2	1/4	3/32	3/64	1/32
#3	1/4	7/64	1/16	3/64
#4	1/4	1/8	1/16	3/64
#5	1/4	1/8	5/64	1/16
#6	5/16	9/64	3/32	5/64
#7	5/16	5/32	3/32	5/64
#8	3/8	11/64	1/8	3/32
#9	3/8	11/64	1/8	3/32
#10	3/8	3/16	1/8	7/64
#11	1/2	3/16	5/32	9/64
#12	1/2	7/32	9/64	1/8

Adhesives

Type	Characteristics	Uses
White glue	**Strength:** moderate; rigid bond **Drying time:** several hours **Resistance to heat:** poor **Resistance to moisture:** poor **Hazards:** none **Cleanup/solvent:** soap and water	**Porous surfaces:** Wood (indoors) Paper Cloth
Yellow glue (carpenter's glue)	**Strength:** moderate to good; rigid bond **Drying time:** several hours; faster than white glue **Resistance to heat:** moderate **Resistance to moisture:** moderate **Hazards:** none **Cleanup/solvent:** soap and water	**Porous surfaces:** Wood (indoors) Paper Cloth
Two-part epoxy	**Strength:** excellent; strongest of all adhesives **Drying time:** varies, depending on manufacturer **Resistance to heat:** excellent **Resistance to moisture:** excellent **Hazards:** fumes are toxic and flammable **Cleanup/solvent:** acetone will dissolve some types	**Smooth & porous surfaces:** Wood (indoors & outdoors) Metal Masonry Glass Fiberglass
Hot glue	**Strength:** depends on type **Drying time:** less than 60 seconds **Resistance to heat:** fair **Resistance to moisture:** good **Hazards:** hot glue can cause burns **Cleanup/solvent:** heat will loosen bond	**Smooth & porous surfaces:** Glass Plastics Wood
Cyanoacrylate (instant glue)	**Strength:** excellent, but with little flexibility **Drying time:** a few seconds **Resistance to heat:** excellent **Resistance to moisture:** excellent **Hazards:** can bond skin instantly; toxic, flammable **Cleanup/solvent:** acetone	**Smooth surfaces:** Glass Ceramics Plastics Metal
Construction adhesive	**Strength:** good to excellent; very durable **Drying time:** 24 hours **Resistance to heat:** good **Resistance to moisture:** excellent **Hazards:** may irritate skin and eyes **Cleanup/solvent:** soap and water (while still wet)	**Porous surfaces:** Framing lumber Plywood and paneling Wallboard Foam panels Masonry
Water-base contact cement	**Strength:** good **Drying time:** bonds instantly; dries fully in 30 minutes **Resistance to heat:** excellent **Resistance to moisture:** good **Hazards:** may irritate skin and eyes **Cleanup/solvent:** soap and water (while still wet)	**Porous surfaces:** Plastic laminates Plywood Flooring Cloth
Silicone sealant (caulk)	**Strength:** fair to good; very flexible bond **Drying time:** 24 hours **Resistance to heat:** good **Resistance to moisture:** excellent **Hazards:** may irritate skin and eyes **Cleanup/solvent:** acetone	**Smooth & porous surfaces:** Wood Ceramics Fiberglass Plastics Glass

Converting Temperatures

Convert degrees Fahrenheit (F) to degrees Celsius (C) by following this simple formula: Subtract 32 from the Fahrenheit temperature reading. Then, mulitply that number by ⅝. For example, 77°F - 32 = 45. 45 × ⅝ = 25°C.

To convert degrees Celsius to degrees Fahrenheit, multiply the Celsius temperature reading by ⅝. Then, add 32. For example, 25°C × ⅝ = 45. 45 + 32 = 77°F.

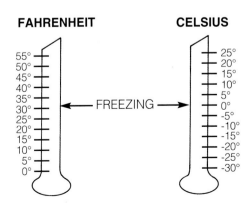

251

Index

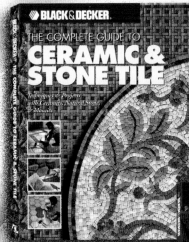
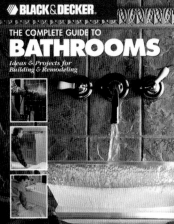
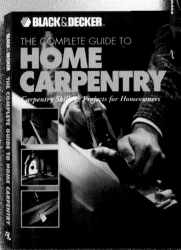